Teaching Shakespeare to Develop Children's Writing

Teaching Shakespeare to Develop Children's Writing

A practical guide: 9–12 years

Fred Sedgwick

Mc Graw Hill Education Open University Press

Open University Press
McGraw-Hill Education
McGraw-Hill House
Shoppenhangers Road
Maidenhead
Berkshire
England
SL6 2QL

email: enquiries@openup.co.uk
world wide web: www.openup.co.uk

and Two Penn Plaza, New York, NY 10121-2289, USA

First published 2014

A catalogue record of this book is available from the British Library

ISBN-13: 978-0-335-26322-6
ISBN-10: 0-335-26322-4
eISBN: 978-0-335-26323-3

Library of Congress Cataloging-in-Publication Data
CIP data applied for

Typeset by Aptara, Inc.

Praise

"Fred Sedgwick has provided a wonderful resource for educators and Shakespeare-lovers alike by allowing us to use the Bard's powerful imagery and timeless characters as spring-boards for creative writing. Not only is this book overflowing with practical lessons, Sedgwick lets his students' work speak for themselves with the inclusion of some highly impressive writing examples from some very young authors."

Sarah Abrams, Education Director, The Shakespeare Society, New York, USA

"With curriculum focus now very much upon grammar and language this book provides a challenging alternative to a text book. The activities cover a range of language and grammatical skills; oxymoron, epithets, kenning, use of punctuation for effect, verb use, identifying parts of speech and so the list goes on.

The careful choices of text not only fulfil curriculum obligation but also engage children in the richness of Shakespeare's language. And, as the examples demonstrate, children can be inspired to engage and experiment with it and consequently enrich their own writing. Who better than the Bard to inspire our children?"

Steve Lott, Head of English, Aldwickbury School, UK

For Daniel (as always)

Contents

List of figures

Acknowledgements

The following schools: Aldwickbury Preparatory, Harpenden; Bealings Primary, Ipswich; Central Park Primary, London; Grundisburgh Primary, Ipswich; Skyswood Primary, St Albans; Springfield Junior, Ipswich; and the Swiss school La Cote International in Vaud.

And, especially, the apprentices at Springfield.

Thanks are due to Sandy Brownjohn for the paraphrase idea in Chapter 14.

Introduction

I have four aims in this book. Here they are in ascending order of importance.

The first is a lowly one, according to the writer in me. **That aim is: to show that when children write in the grip of Shakespeare's language, his lines have the potential to help children to improve their 'literacy skills'.** When you teach his plays, William Shakespeare will walk around your classroom, just as you do when the children write.

To put the matter at a higher level, an engagement with the complexities of Shakespeare's verse and prose – his way with metre, dialogue, characterisation, simile, metaphor, sentence structure – his way with language – offers opportunities for children to use their own language to describe, inform, persuade and give pleasure. To be gripped while still young by Shakespeare's language, and by the language of other writers who will inevitably follow if teachers are willing and enthusiastic enough to use literature in their English lessons is to be set up for life with an enlivening and (above all, I think) a delight-generating skill.

It would have seemed strange to Shakespeare to have heard his words spoken in classrooms, and to have seen children writing under the influence of them. But he experienced the same power in the Latin poets and the Latin and English historians he was taught by at Stratford Grammar School. And he also experienced the power of the Bible he heard and read both at school and in Holy Trinity Church in his home town, Stratford, and in whichever church he worshipped in when working in Southwark. We know this from the plays: when still very young he wrote the terrifying *Titus Andronicus*: Ovid's lines lurk not very deep underneath his.

And *The Book of Job* haunts *Timon of Athens*. Perhaps the strangest example of biblical influence is in *A Midsummer Night's Dream*. Imagine a pub quiz question: which Shakespeare character misquotes St Paul's *First Letter to the Corinthians*? Here is Paul in Chapter 2 verse 9:

Eye hath not seen, nor ear heard, neither have entered into the heart of man, the things which God hath prepared for them that love him . . .

and here is Bottom (yes it's him!) in The *Dream* Act 4 Scene 1:

> The eye of man hath not heard, the ear of man hath not seen, man's hand is not able to taste, his tongue to conceive, not his heart to report what my dream was!

Shakespeare's teachers gave him the power of words through literature, and to deprive children of the opportunity for intense study and delight in Shakespeare's would be a sin.

I'll come back to that word 'delight' later.

The second aim I have in this book: I want to try to counter ways of teaching Shakespeare that miss the whole point, which is, as I am insisting, his language

One traditional practice, probably started by Charles and Mary Lamb in their book *Tales from Shakespeare* (1994[1807]), is the telling of the stories to children as though they were Shakespeare's work; as though recounting the plots equals teaching Shakespeare.

When I was a primary school head teacher I watched a man in a primary assembly spend about half an hour of his life going through the whole plot of *Macbeth*. The children, aged from five to eleven, stared at him in silence, much as they might have stared at a man dancing the polka in the shopping centre. (It was half an hour out of their lives too, I remember reflecting sourly.) It is the only example of discipline by mesmerisation I have encountered. He had been a head of an English department in a secondary school, but if he knew that the plot of this play was not Shakespeare's, he didn't care. In fact, only two of the plots were actually made up by Shakespeare: the rest come from various sources, some of which I've already mentioned.

It is not as though Shakespeare was unique in his lifting of stories: there were almost always sources behind the stories in Elizabethan plays. If one of Shakespeare's skills is story-telling, and of course it is, he manifests it through the shaping of his acts and scenes, through his language and the way it betrays a character's thoughts and emotions – and not through his putting together of bare bones of the plot. Having said all that, I have given brief plot summaries at the beginning of each section: some might find them helpful.

My third aim is to present Shakespeare to the young before sentimental errors take root in their minds

The advertising and the public relations industries have planted false notions of Shakespeare in the minds of all English speakers. Some examples: even though the 'weird sisters' in *Macbeth* are only once called 'witches' in the play, and even though they are no longer presented on stage with that black paraphernalia – headgear, broomsticks and cats – that is how they are still seen in the public imagination. They are, far more troublingly to my ear anyway, 'weird sisters' in *Macbeth*. That phrase, Shakespeare's, is profoundly disturbing to children, as well: however far sibling rivalry goes in a family, 'weird sister' will always sound like a (possibly facetious?) oxymoron. And Juliet didn't look out over a balcony, like the woman in the chocolate advertisement of a few years ago; and when she said 'Wherefore art thou Romeo?' she wasn't looking for him, but rhetorically wishing he wasn't a member of the Montague family 'Why are you Romeo *Montague*?'

Then there are Titania's servants in The *Dream* presented as the fluttering fairies of a Victorian girl's fantasy. And, pre-eminently, perhaps, there's Hamlet, the young brooding, moody student prince in white doublet and black hose meditatively holding a skull, and in need of the calming cigar that bears his name.

There are the first three of the four main aims I have in this book: to help children to learn their language (literacy in today-speak); to combat a pedagogy that relies on the plots rather than the language; and to counter sentimental views of him and his work. As the first is a relatively low-level one, at least as far as I'm concerned, and as the second and third have a negative slant, the rest of the introduction gives some idea of what I take to be the positive value of teaching Shakespeare to young children.

My fourth aim is to show how Shakespeare's lines can give delight to teachers and children when they work together with him

I am going to define 'delight' in a broad sense. I use it here to attempt to describe the pleasure or joy (both these words are inadequate, of course) that goes through us when we see art and think: that's right, I know something of that, I recognise it, now take me further. As Vladimir Nabokov wrote in his *Lectures on Literature* (1980):

> Although we read with our minds, the seat of artistic delight is between the shoulder blades. That little shiver behind is quite certainly the highest form of emotion that humanity has attained when evolving pure art and pure science . . .

For me, that delight in words does not manifest itself where it did for Nabokov, but I still know what he means. And, more to the point, I have seen some evidence of it many times in children's eyes: I have watched their faces as they hear Puck's lines 'I'll follow you' from The *Dream* (see Lesson Seven). It is also there in the tension in their bodies, a stillness at such variance to the default mode of childhood, the forward-leaning dash on field or playground. There is delight in their eyes in the old sense, but also something different and far deeper inside each one of them when he or she asks him/herself, 'How does Puck change himself into fire, or a horse? What will he do to Bottom when he's caught him? How will I write more lines for Puck to say?'

This delight in language: a personal example. When I was in the sixth form of my London school, a master took a group of boys to see *Henry IV Part 1* at the Old Vic. I heard this exchange, and looked it up later:

> FALSTAFF Now, Hal, what time of day is it, lad?
>
> PRINCE Thou art so fat-witted with drinking of old sack, and unbut-
> toning thee after supper, and sleeping upon benches after noon, thou
> hast forgotten to demand that truly which thou would truly know.
> What a devil hast thou to do with the time of day? Unless hours were
> cups of sack, and minutes capons, and clocks the tongues of bawds,
> and dials the signs of leaping houses, and the blessed sun herself a fair
> hot wench in flame-coloured taffeta, I see no reason why thou shouldst
> be so superfluous to demand the time of day.

'Sack', 'capons', 'bawds', 'leaping houses', 'wench', 'taffeta': I knew nothing of the meanings of these words; but the sound of them, and the rhythm, rising in a crescendo to that climax about the blessed sun and (especially, especially) that 'fair hot wench' (I think I could infer what *that* meant) . . . I was entranced. Or, I would say now, delighted.

Shakespeare's work is, as the director Deborah Warner has written, 'a benign and tolerant celebration of the human', and delighting in him is part of delighting in what it is to be human.

Through all the vagaries of different versions of the National Curriculum, Shakespeare's name is a constant; and it is our bounden duty (and it should be our joy) as teachers to offer his words to children in as vibrant manner as we can. In past times, the task of introducing Shakespeare's work has fallen on teachers in secondary schools. But children from nine years old upwards can draw inspiration from his words.

Getting a grip on Shakespeare's words is one way in which young children can begin to make sense of their lives today. In this book, I will give examples of them doing this by their talking about them; by their acting parts of scenes, whether as 'radio plays' (that is, with voices only) or with actions in larger spaces than the classroom; by their designing costumes for certain characters; but, in the main, by their writing in the grip of those words. Shakespeare addresses the central issues of being a human being, both as an individual and in society, more profoundly than any other single writer; and he does it in the way of a genius.

Harold Bloom surely exaggerates when he writes in his 1999 book that Shakespeare 'invented' for Western man the notion of the human being, but it is not difficult to see and appreciate what his hyperbole is driving at. Here, for the first time, characters examine themselves alive and aloud on stage, and thereby expose their thoughts and feelings to us ('O! what a rogue and peasant slave am I!') and, by doing so, at one remove, expose ourselves to ourselves. Shakespeare's words prepare us all, if we let them, for the slings and arrows of outrageous fortune far more effectively than any lifestyle manual. And in doing so, if we give them time and study, they will delight both us and our children.

There are comments on teaching Shakespeare in an international context in Note A at the end of the book.

All the writing is by children in mixed-ability classes except where otherwise described. 'The apprentices' are a loose group of gifted and (rather more to the point as far as I'm concerned) keen writers aged from eight to eleven years in Springfield Junior School, Ipswich. I have been meeting the group for nearly three years, and I still do, though children have left, mostly to go to secondary school, and every year new children arrive.

References to lines in the plays are given thus: 3.4.20–30 means Act 3 Scene 4 lines 20–30.

All boxed areas are practical activities.

1 Two simple ways into Shakespeare's Language: Similes and oxymorons

Lesson One: Like to a silver bow

In this lesson there are similes from three places in Shakespeare's work: *A Midsummer Night's Dream, The Tempest* and *The Sonnets.* It is at the beginning because it presents no problem in the teaching of it.

By the time they're eight or nine years old, most children are used to similes. Even if they can't identify them as such, they have come across them in conversations with their parents, on television, and in their reading. Like all great writers, Shakespeare uses vivid examples habitually, so to begin with them offers an entry point to the study of his plays; and to literature; and, in fact, to language in general.

 Revise briefly what a simile is. Then point out these two easily visualised examples and write them up:

And then the moon, like to a silver bow
New bent in heaven . . .

That's part of Hippolyta's first speech in 1:1, spoken while she is anticipating her marriage to Theseus.

Ask the children: is this a simile or a metaphor? It's a simile, of course, because the comparison is made explicit by the word 'like'. A metaphor would have been 'then the moon, a silver bow . . .' Draw a crescent moon on the board with a bow inside it, and mime the bowman.

1

Ask the children to make similes from one sphere of reference, the sky. You could offer these as examples – they're by ten-year-olds – and then ask them to distinguish simile from metaphor:

- *Distant stars float by like the sequins on a girl's best dress.*
- *The moon sails like an old wrecked ship sailing the spiralled clouds.*
- *Trees shade over misty clouds like cross-hatching on paper.*
- *Shiny sequins of the sky, the broken glass of a precious moon.*

Note, by the way, that these children were not only already familiar with the *definition* of alliteration (an easy matter! – a repetition of consonantal sounds); they were also accustomed to using it in their writing. Play with the sounds that language makes, which begins in the earliest years, should become a daily event.

Ask them to find other similes in the play. Lysander is fond of them. Love is (he says):

. . . momentany [momentary] as a sound,
Swift as a shadow, short as any dream,
Brief as the lightning in the collied [coal-black] night . . .

(I.I.144–146)

And Demetrius sends out a volley of exaggerated examples at 3.2.137, beginning 'O Helen, goddess . . .' More of his similes in Part 1.

As free / As mountain winds

'As' works in similes too. In 1.2.498–499, Prospero uses a simile for freedom: he promises Ariel that he will be 'as free / As mountain winds'.

Ask the children to close their eyes and think of further similes for freedom that use the word 'as' . . . Insist that they get four or five before offering any to the rest of the class.

I asked a class of eight-year-olds to think of some similes about freedom along these lines. The frame was 'I shall be free as . . .' They offered:

- *seagulls flying*
- *the ocean swaying*
- *a wild horse cantering*
- *clouds floating*
- *a wild wolf*
- *nature flying through the world*
- *the stars shining*
- *a stormy night*
- *a hovering hawk*
- *a whispering ocean*
- *a midnight owl*
- *the whimpering wind*
- *every breath you take*
- *a meteor in space*
- *a lost kite.*

I told them, briefly, how Ariel, a character in *The Tempest*, had been imprisoned in a tree, and asked them for further similes for trapped or imprisoned:

- *as a beetle in a Venus Fly Trap*
- *as an ant in ice*
- *as lead in a pencil*
- *as light in a sunset.*

Like to the lark at break of day arriving

I doubt whether the Sonnets are taught very often in primary schools. But I think some children might be grateful one day for having been introduced to this simile. In Sonnet 29, Shakespeare says that he is 'in disgrace with Fortune and men's eyes' – until he thinks of his love. And then his state

Like to the lark at break of day arising
From sullen earth sings hymns at heaven's gate.

> Read these lines. Describe the way a skylark suddenly climbs the air in a vertical line, hammering out the song as it rises, and continuing to do so when it is almost out of sight . . . And then still singing! If the children are accustomed to listening to music, you could play a recording of Ralph Vaughan Williams' *The Lark Ascending*, where the solo violin imitates the movement of the bird, climaxing twice, once after five minutes, again in the final fourteenth: you can hear the bird hammering the sky.
>
> What a simile for pure joy this is! Ask the children to think of similes for any happiness that comes on them suddenly – when they see an uncle or aunt they haven't seen for a long time, or when they realise it's the first day of the holidays.

Here are some examples from my first session using this poem with children. They were members of a class of eight-year-olds.

I feel

- *as upbeat as R & B*
- *like when I've found the missing piece of the jigsaw puzzle*
- *like leaves changing into blossom*
- *that I am right at the top of the loudest scream.*

For another much more demanding lesson based on a Shakespeare sonnet, see the last one in this book.

Lesson Two: Such sweet thunder

That sub-title is an oxymoron: a phrase that seems to contradict itself. It's a line from *A Midsummer Night's Dream* (4.1.115), a play that was written when Shakespeare was in his twenties or possibly his early thirties. It has often been noted that the phrase sums up the plot of the play. As a young writer, Shakespeare used oxymorons to powerful effect. In *Romeo and Juliet* they're sometimes packed together in single speeches. There is a lesson in Part 3 about two moments of crisis where this happens (Romeo at 1.1.167–173, bemoaning his unrequited love for Rosaline, and Juliet at 3.2.73–79 after she hears the news that her lover has killed her cousin). Juliet utters one of the most famous when she says to Romeo at the end of 2.2. 'Parting is such sweet sorrow'. This shared linguistic trick is one of the ways in which Shakespeare shows us how close the lovers are.

In The *Dream* Hippolyta has two oxymorons jammed up against each other as she describes the sound of howling dogs: 'So musical a discord, such sweet thunder'.

> Explain 'discord'. Prepare some oxymorons of your own. Don't be afraid of banality: 'wooden car', 'square wheel' will serve the purpose to begin with. Then ask the children to write their own. Theirs too will be dull at first. But, as a second stage, you might ask the children to restrict their attempts to another subject in the curriculum.

Here are some musical examples from ten-year-olds:

A broken melody.
A ruined rhythm.
A stringed trombone.
A tuneless symphony.
A wobbly rhythm.
A soundless harmony.

A keyless piano.
A stringless guitar.
A noteless tune.
A wordless song.
A deep deep soprano.

These eight-years-olds had been studying volcanoes, and there was evidence about the room – paintings, notes taken while watching a DVD, reference books open at pages describing and depicting eruptions – that they knew a great deal about Pompeii. They wrote, among others:

> *Beautiful ash clouds.*
> *Tremendous pumice.*
> *Friendly ash.*
> *Honey rock.*
> *Flowery volcano.*
> *Cotton candy ash clouds.*
> *Snowy volcano.*

Then ask the children, if you think they are ready for it (in Years five and six, some of them certainly will be), to use abstract nouns. These are from my apprentices:

> *Loathsome love.*
> *Hopeful loneliness.*
> *Living death.*
> *Dead imagination.*
> *Peaceful hatred.*

Any topic is open to the making of oxymorons. Try maths ('shaky symmetry') or history ('gentle warfare') or geography ('icy desert', 'sandy tundra', 'rich Africa').

For enthusiastic students, you might set this task. Near the beginning of the second scene of *Hamlet*, Claudius is speaking to his courtiers, and his oxymorons arguably tell us a lot about him: 'defeated joy', 'mirth in funeral', 'dirge in marriage', 'delight and dole'. Ask them to find them. Discuss what they might suggest about his character. There is, perhaps, something of the double man; he's a sayer of two things at once; is someone to be trusted who can talk of 'dirge in marriage' just after his wedding? Then ask them to write oxymorons that are dark in colour, like those.

There's much more on oxymorons later in Part 3.

A Local Habitation: A Midsummer Night's Dream

A Summary

There are four worlds in *A Midsummer Night's Dream*. The first is the court, where Theseus, who has just defeated Hippolyta in war (will the course of *that* love run smooth there?) is preparing to marry her. The second world comprises the lovers. Hermia, contrary to her father's wishes, is in love with Lysander when the play begins, and Helena in love with Demetrius, who loves Hermia. These loves will be confused by Puck's potion, which he fetches on Oberon's orders, and on which much of the play depends.

The third world is that of six workmen from the city of Athens, traditionally known as the mechanicals, who are rehearsing a play that they will present to the first two worlds at the end. Peter Quince is in charge when Bottom lets him be, which is occasionally.

The last world is that of the fairies, the king Oberon and the queen Titania. They have fallen out over 'a little Indian boy', whom they both want to possess. The king has his servant Puck and the queen has her fairies.

These four worlds collide at certain points in the play – first in 2.2, when Puck's potion sets the four young lovers at sixes and sevens; and then, in 3.1 when the same potion befuddles the queen Titania and Bottom.

The summary summarised:

The course of true love never did run smooth.
(Lysander in 1.1.134)

This part of my book contains lessons which focus on the main characters in the *Dream*: first, a character that children seem to have an instinctive empathy with, Puck; and then Bottom and his friends; then Titania and her servants; and finally the lovers.

There are two main reasons why this play works so well in primary classrooms – two at least to be going along with. There's the humour: Shakespeare's jokes in other plays may fall flat on ears that are not attuned to his language, but it would be an unimaginably dreary production of The *Dream* that did not raise laughs when Bottom and his friends are on stage. And there's the theme, which has a pretty much universal interest. Love matters to everyone, whether it's running smooth or rough.

Puck and Bottom matter most; more importantly for my purposes as a teacher, they matter most to children. Certainly, the four lovers, Lysander, Demetrius, Hermia and Helena are funny, especially the girls in their cat-fighting: Hermia, the short one, and Helena, the tall one (3:2, and see Chapter 5, Lesson Twenty-Seven); but they're also just silly: the boys, Demetrius and Lysander, fickle and quarrelsome, are entirely at the bidding of Puck's potion and their own machismo. Helena talks too much – listen to her at the end of 1.1 as she ponders the subject of love. And all four of them are still some way beyond the children's ken.

But Bottom and Puck: if the children get a grip on these two individuals, they will have the beginnings of an understanding of the play. There are so many ways that Puck, especially, can trick children into writing; to 'trip' them, in Seamus Heaney's phrase about creative writing, 'to fall into themselves unknowingly' ('The Play Way' in Heaney 1966). And that tripping will be falling into understanding about The *Dream* as well as about themselves.

For more on them, and the way they can relate to children, see Note B.

2 'That merry wanderer'
Mostly Puck

Lesson Three: Slipping from her bum

 Read these lines:

I am that merry wanderer of the night.
I jest to Oberon and make him smile
When I a fat and bean-fed horse beguile,
Neighing in likeness of a filly foal;
And sometime lurk I in a gossip's bowl
In very likeness of a roasted crab,
And when she drinks, against her lips I bob,
And on her weathered dewlap pour the ale.
The wisest aunt, telling the saddest tale,
Sometime for threefoot stool mistaketh me;
Then slip I from her bum, down topples she . . .

                                        2:1:43–51

Act them as best you can, taking hints from the language: 'wanderer', 'lurk', 'pour', 'topples' etc. You might also read them the lines that appear on p. 21 ('I'll follow you . . .' from 3.1), and those on p. 28–9 ('Now the hungry lion roars' from 5.2) as well as the simile from Lesson One above. Although these passages are not necessary at this stage, if you do read them, your children will have begun to know Puck very well.

> Ask the children to come up with adjectives, nouns and phrases 'that say something about Puck's character'.

A group of writers identified by their school as 'gifted', by me as 'keen' and by one of them as my 'apprentices' came up quickly with these, among others:

flexible, sly, disloyal, riddlesome, nasty, intelligent, hardcore, crazy, a pest, irritating, swift, sneaky, merry, meddlesome, cunning, elegant, versatile, nocturnal, humorous, sinister, dark, trying, nimble, misleading, agile, swift, ingenious, on his toes, adventurous, fluid, delicate, sly, a trickster, quick, a shape-shifter, a stalker, infuriating, stealthy, evil, cheerful, clever, running, a flier, annoying, curious.

Lesson Four: Merry wanderer

Read 'I am that merry wanderer' again. Become Puck in the classroom. All the preparation this involves is some mental picturing of the images, like that of the fat horse fooled by Puck's imitation of a filly's whinny, that crab in a bowl of ale bobbing against the old woman's mouth, that three-legged stool shifting as she sits and a relishing of the words: 'lurk', 'drink', 'bum'. It's a help if you have something of the child in you, as Puck and Bottom both do.

Many of the difficult images (that 'bean-fed horse', that 'filly foal', that 'dewlap') can be, if not acted, looked up or explained quickly. Then talk about Puck and his behaviour, using the adjectives they have suggested as a framework. Sometimes you might do this as a class; sometimes, the children might work in small groups of five or six and then share ideas as a whole class later. Then, ask the children to write lines for their Puck character. Always, the children should understand that they might be asked to read or even perform their words to their friends.

Here is some work by the group of able writers I've referred to above:

I am that mischievous man
of the night
cutting down branches
and leaving guiltily everywhere
around me.
I am nonsense
to the whole forest
in the dead of night.
Things get ruined
by me.
I am a dreadful person
and I always will be.

I am a disturbing man
that will never let you
finish your sentences.
I am that mischievous man
of the night.

Charlie

Charlie's line breaks, at least towards the beginning of the piece, are fitting, and he rounds his poem off neatly by repeating his opening lines. In the next example, the beginning of the second line is chilling, and then the fourth line introduces a knowing example of bathos. But, more importantly, Lottie has internalised some of Shakespeare's rhythm, and her previous experience of poetry, relatively wide for a nine-year-old, has been in the back of her mind:

I am the one who burns you down to a crisp,
the tap on your shoulder, the spicy hot fire.

I am the one who smashed the window and shot
your father in the face! - with a sponge ball!

I was the one who invented eating snails.
I am the one who took away your friends,
the evil not going away.

I am the one that makes you lost, that never-ending
trail stuck to your mind.

I am the one forcing you to do bad things
although I never get away with it.

Lottie

The first line of that piece has five beats: I AM the ONE who BURNS you DOWN to a CRISP (though the natural speaking voice will downplay the first, on 'am' – transferring it back to 'I') and the second has four: the TAP on your SHOULder, the SPIcy hot FIRE . . .

It is important to make it clear that Lottie has learned this without being explicitly taught it. She has, to put it a better way, breathed in Shakespeare's rhythm in the classroom. Not everything that is learned can, or must, be taught. Children learn about rhythm and metre without necessarily knowing those technical words, much as someone ignorant of the words 'love', 'joy', 'delight' and 'thrill' can still experience those emotions and sensations; and much as we all use thousands of verbs before we can define the word 'verb', and millions of phonemes before we can define 'phoneme'.

This writing also allows children the pleasure of wish-fulfilment: Charlie and Lottie would, almost certainly, never be as naughty as this, but dreaming about mischief in words inspired by Puck's is a delight. It is an *innocent transgression*, a *safe trespass* (oxymorons – see Lesson One, and *Romeo and Juliet* later – can be catching) and has set them free to write with purpose, and to write with purpose is to improve one's literacy.

In another school, a group of eight- and nine-year-olds spent longer on the Puck exercise. None of the children had been labelled by the school as 'gifted', though several of them were, as in all classes.

The headteacher had told me that there were several boys in the class who found writing difficult. And so while teaching I focussed, laser-like, on them. Floyd produced a fascinating document, but there is no space to say much about it here, except to say that this is how it ended up, edited (quite lightly):

I am the God of mischief.
I explode drinks
in children's faces.
I play pranks on babies
and I hide their things.
That's the reason I'm banned from the spirit world.

I am as sneaky as God.
I flood people's houses.
I blow up people's houses
when they're away.
That's why I am banned from the spirit world.

Floyd

Another boy, Joe, wrote:

> I am the mystery presence
> that lurks around by the trees at night.
> Some people call me the beast of 20,000 leagues
> Some people call me the shadow of the night
> I fire a gun to frighten
> People around me
>
> Joe

He stalled here: see Note C for what happened next.

See for comparison the writing by two girls, Nina and Alba:

> I am that troubled maker of weather.
> I make thunder, lightning and storms.
> I can make waves with my power and
> Wreck the sand sculptures that the artists make.
>
> Boats and ships
> Watch out!
> Storms might pass by.
>
> I can flood plants with storms.
> I can make drought. I can make
> Antarctica the hottest continent in the world
> And Africa the coldest.
>
> The rain forest!!!
> I can make it the drought forest.
> I can make the sun move to the other
> Side of the world. Plants that need
> Sun might die. Summer might never come.
> It could be winter for the rest of your life.
> I can make the weather for my friend, storms, hurricanes,

Flood, drought and flash floods.
I am that troubled maker of weather.
> *Nina*

There is such fluency evident in this writing. She attacks the task with a confidence that was visible in the pace at which she wrote, and is still visible in the layout she uses, and in the way (always encouraging, this) that she employs knowledge she has acquired in other areas of the curriculum. And there is adventurousness here: 'Storms might pass by'. Indeed, anything might happen and probably would have happened had she not been restricted to half an hour. Note that trick of finishing her piece with the line that began it. Here is Alba's work:

I am that naughty beach man
Who smashes sandcastles down
That have been made by the children.
I put seawater in their drinks.
I put live fish in their sandwiches.
I put sand on top of their parents that are sleeping.
I put slimy seaweed into ladies' handbags.
I go into their huts and fiddle with their things.
I make the sea waves come and wash everything.
> *Alba*

I have made a point in my introduction that Shakespeare is the inheritance, potentially, of all people. I always ask bilingual writers, such as Alba, if they would like to translate their work, or part of it, into their other, in this case, first, language. Alba was very willing, and wrote down quickly in Spanish, beginning 'Yo soy la nina mala de sa playa / Que rompe castillos de arena . . .'

There is an ever-increasing number of children in our schools who can write in two languages, and when I meet them, I feel (as someone brought up and educated as a monoglot) a responsibility to help them to keep a hold on that ability.

Lesson Five: Meeting Puck in the forest

This is such a simple way of writing about Puck.

> When the children are familiar with some of his words, say a line from Jacques in *As You Like It* (2.7.12): 'A fool, a fool! I met a fool i' the forest . . .' Then revise some of Puck's lines above, and ask the children to begin poems beginning with Jacques' line or something like it – but their poems must be about Puck.

These examples are from the apprentices:

I met Puck in the forest:
He's like an irritating fly
That you can never get rid of.

I met Puck in the forest:
He ambushed a badger by shape-shifting
Into an eagle, flew down and scared
The badger away into darkness.

That's what I thought!

A while later Puck darted through
The brambles and bushes and trees,
A sinister smile planted on his sly face.

He had broken a pot
As an old a feeble woman held a grey tartan vase
In her withered hands.

That is by Ruby, who is nine years old. She has taken the shape-shifting idea from Puck's changeable behaviour as described by himself in both the 'Merry Wanderer' speech in Lesson Three and the 'I'll follow you' speech in Lesson Seven, and she has taken her line length from his cadences. I find it hard, though it's interesting to try, to visualise a 'grey tartan vase', but I think that 'smile planted on his sly face' is perfect.

I met Puck in the forest. He is an evil trickster of the night. & master of shadows a star of many nightmares. His soul is twisted and damaged. If it, that is Puck, I mean, had a soul. No love has changed. So now his solemn duty is to spread evil and chaos sprinkled with sadness of the sour kind. He is a disease but means to be a cold.

Ayesha

Lesson Six: A girdle round about the earth

> I'll put a girdle round about the earth
> In forty minutes!

So says Puck to Oberon 2:1:175. The fairy king has just given him his orders:

> Fetch me that flower, the herb I showed thee once;
> The juice of it on sleeping eyelids laid
> Will make a man or woman madly dote
> Upon the next live creature that it sees.

Later, at 3.2.100, Oberon tells Puck to find 'Helena of Athens' so that he can undo the mischief. Puck says (as we have seen in Chapter 1):

> I go, I go, look how I go!
> Swifter than arrow from the Tartar's bow.

Often we need no more than a line or two to get children writing.

You might revise 'I am that merry wanderer' (Lesson Four) and read 'I'll follow you' (Lesson Seven). Act the lines that climax in the Tartar's bow, pointing out that the phrase 'round about' in the first quotation has something in it that is like the roundness of the earth; and that the repetition of the 'o' sounds in the second help the lines to race along as Puck is promising Oberon he will do as he's been ordered. Those repeated 'O' sounds are the shape of one of Shakespeare's theatres.

This lesson could be linked to some history. In Shakespeare's time, the idea of circumnavigating the globe was relatively new: in 1522, forty-two years before Shakespeare's birth, a remnant of Ferdinand Magellan's 1519 expedition (without their leader, killed in a fight four months before) finished the first circumnavigation of the world. The 'Globe' as a name for a theatre would have been unthinkable in the previous century; now, it caught the flavour of the times. So Puck's words here would have had a topical significance, and the more educated of his hearers would have nodded knowingly at each other: Puck is a Magellan.

Ask the children to re-write those words, bringing them up to date. Suggest that they use other consonantal and vowel sounds that are suitable to Puck's movement. Examples in the work below are the repeated 'ck' sounds in Danielle's lines; the long 'I/fly/glide/slide' sounds in Eleanor's and Katie's, as well as the latter's repeated 'ing' sounds; the 'soar/storm' assonance in Mia's – all this and more show how they have learned another lesson from playing with Shakespeare's technique.

These children are nine- and ten-year-olds:

I'll shoot a plane around the world
And move as quick as a wink.
                    Danielle

I'll move, I'll fly, I'll leap up to their eye,
I'll glide and slide.
                    Eleanor

I'll fly, I'll fly, soar, swoop and swerve, skimming the water,
brushing the mountain tops.
                    Katie

I'll soar, I'll soar,
Faster than a rocket at top speed
As fast as a wave during a storm.
                    Mia

I'll sprint, jump, gallop, all the way
Till I find the drink, quick as a click!

Ruby

I'm gone in seconds, I will rush,
Crush your mind to find what you think.

Lottie

Lesson Seven: Sometime a horse I'll be, sometime a hound

I'll follow you: I'll lead you about a round,
　　Through bog, through bush, through brake, through briar;
Sometime a horse I'll be, sometime a hound,
　　A hog, a headless bear, sometime a fire,
And neigh, and bark, and grunt, and roar, and burn,
Like horse, hound, hog, bear, fire at every turn.

3:1:88–93

These lines of Puck's make up my 'Model T' Shakespeare lesson, the first I thought of, designed, built and drove in a classroom. As I've said in Lesson One, I had discovered long ago that, contrary to most people's thinking, Shakespeare is not at all difficult for children: note that, in these lines, only one word – 'brake' – needs explaining. Here was a speech that exemplified that approachability, and I have taught it hundreds of times, sometimes with children as young as six years old.

My lessons are not intended to be recipes to be strictly followed. They are more like launching pads for further ideas. Nevertheless, this is how I recommend teaching 'I'll follow you':

> ➤ Tell them that Puck has just come into the room and they are about to hear him speak. Then say the lines as well as you can, trying to emphasise certain traits to the character. It makes a difference if you can speak the script rather than read it – just keep a copy of the play near at hand as a prompt book.
>
> 　The lines require, among other things, a slightly threatening tone, a nimbleness, a playfulness. Many of the movements Shakespeare wanted from his actors are implicit in the speeches, especially in their punctuation. Here, make a very long pause at that colon in line 1, and other pauses, still quite long, at

all the semi-colons and commas. Try to hint with your voice at the animals in line 5, and at flames when you say 'burn'. If you know the class well, approach individuals or groups on certain phrases, pretending to threaten them. (There are further suggestions for teaching these lines in Note D.)

Puck's words are all about a midsummer night forest, of course. Invite the children to think about different environments. The more different their choices are from Puck's, the better their writing will be. Collect some suggestions on the board. You could start them off with these: a supermarket, a church, a park, the solar system, the town centre, a Greek island, a zoo, under the sea, inside a volcano, the public library, a place they've visited on holiday, a farm . . .

You could suggest places from their reading, and they often come up with Hogwarts school. Then draw in the topics in science and history that they have been studying: I have noted before how satisfying and educational it is when work in poetry and Shakespeare impinges on the rest of the curriculum, and vice versa: the human body, Tudor England, World War I, a Victorian town, an orchestra, a laboratory, an artist, a volcano, a car engine . . .

Suggest that they use environments that arise from their own passions, such as music, sport and so on. Collect from the children as many prepositions and prepositional phrases as they can muster – 'before', 'under', 'below', 'behind', 'over', 'through', 'round', 'in front of', 'at the back of', and so on, and also suggest that beginning the lines occasionally with 'where' will make their writing stronger, because it's a word that opens up further possibilities. It acts like a key, opening new possibilities. This is especially true for inexperienced writers.

This boy, in a class of nine-year-olds, decided to set his poem inside a computer. He has found the word 'where' liberating, and a Puckish stalker is present in his writing. Which is exactly what, as a teacher, I treasure: Shakespeare's words are sensed like a ghost in a twenty-first century boy's words:

> I'll follow you
> in the circuit boards
> where the power grows.
> I'll follow you
> under the wires

where messages
are sent through
a never-ending cycle.
I'll follow you
through a speaker
where a sound
opens up.
I'll follow you
within the computer
where ideas become
a presentation.
I'll follow you
between the printers
where the cartridges
die.
I'll follow you
over the keyboards
where you see
only brown stains.
                    Johnnie

Esme (10) was one of the apprentices. She can punctuate with conventional accuracy, as Johnnie has there. So her decision in the next piece to do without commas and full stops is both deliberate and appropriate for the rapid flowing movement. I had taken this group to two art galleries earlier in the term, though Esme's imagination has led her to see things ('discarded canvasses', for example) that we didn't see:

I'll follow you
through swivelling glass doors
to an art gallery
I'll follow you
in and out of
shining marble sculptures

I'll follow you
down a secret staircase
where discarded canvasses lie
I'll follow you
to a room full of
towering gold frames
holding pictures of someone
being followed
I'll follow you
around about the hidden rooms
where people stare at you
with unblinking eyes
I'll follow you
to the exit
on the bus
round the corner and home again
I'll follow you

Esme

This is mature writing. There is an earlier draft of this in front of me, and it is interesting to note that Esme has had the confidence to dump the grown-up sounding clause 'as I relentlessly follow you', with its unnecessary adverb. And I enjoy the clever internal reference, 'pictures of someone / being followed' and those 'people [who] stare at you/with unblinking eyes'. Are they other visitors to the gallery or in the subjects in the pictures?

Ruby had looked at a statue of a ballerina that resembled in some ways the work of Degas. So she used her enthusiasm for, and knowledge of, ballet:

I'll follow you
underneath the barre
where legs bend
and demi plie.
around the wings

where dancers
wait for their cue.

I'll follow you
behind the stage
where trapdoors
lie open
between can-canning ladies
where roses are thrown.

I'll follow you
within dressing tables
where make-up is being applied
out of chasse
where spring points
change and point.

I'll follow you
over rond de jambe
and ballonse
where arms
float delicately.

Ruby

Some years ago, a boy, ten years old, wrote something under the influence of Shakespeare's lines for Puck, and this lesson, that still delights me with its inventiveness and playfulness. Children playing behave like creative writers, making worlds of their own:

I'll follow you
though the A's and B's
where antelopes accompany bears.
I'll follow you

up and around C's and D's
dancing and drifting around cloakrooms.
I'll follow you
under economy and over faucets and fax machines
that collect geese and gloves and grates.
I'll follow you
where hammers and hamburgers hastily chase you,
to where infants invent ingenious illusions next to J
where juggernauts journey to Jersey
where kings and kitchen are in K.
Light and lifts light up L
and money menaces M
and naughty gnomes knock on N.
I'll follow you
over octopuses, olives and oxen.
P's and Q's
Practise pranks in the queen's quiet chambers and
R and S follow
for spider races in Supercross speedway.
Tarantulas terrorise tourists in tea that comes from Turkey.
I'll follow you
past unities and umbrellas in U
and violins vigorously play a Viking tune.
We wish we could weave well from W
and see X-rays and xylophones in X.
I'll follow you
through Y and Z
zigzagging through zones of life.
I will follow you—
from beginning to end.
I'll follow you

Ryan

Lesson Eight: I'll follow you – Drama

You could make a drama lesson of this speech. For this you need the hall or gym, or in fine summer weather among trees you could find an exactly appropriate setting. The children should work in pairs, first of all practising ways of saying their lines, alternating with each other. I use here Ruby's poem above as an example.

Ayesha might say 'I'll follow you / past Leonardo / the helicopter inventor' and Ruby might respond with 'I'll follow you / behind the stage / where trapdoors / lie open / where roses are thrown' and then Ayesha puts in more lines and so on until both sets of lines are used up. If one reader has more lines than the other, the second could be 'commissioned' to write more for her contribution.

Then, once the children have their lines more or less by heart, they should prepare movements to suit them with their whole bodies, trying to keep in contact with each other, swooping down and then up, going round to the other side of the partner to startle her.

Finally, you might ask them to prepare dramatic little productions with Shakespeare's own words which are, as I've written earlier, so full of stage directions: 'follow', 'lead', 'around about', 'horse', 'fire' and so on.

If you can find another class to be an audience for these productions, so much the better: drama needs its audience.

Lesson Nine: Now the hungry lion roars

This passage at 5:1:349–368 is, among other things, a lyric poem about night-time. The exhausted ploughman, the screeching owl and 'the church-way paths' where sprites 'glide' place it in Shakespeare's England – especially, probably, his native Warwickshire; but the lion and the wolves give it a more exotic and a more dangerous setting. The poem is also about saying goodbye, to a day of course, but also, or perhaps, to a life: you can read 'weary task foredone' both ways, and the churchyards, the sprites and the shrouds underline this sense of threat.

And that homely ending! Is Puck sweeping merely the dust that is behind the door, or sweeping all the dust in the room behind that door, so that Master and Mistress won't see it?

> Now the hungry lion roars,
>   And the wolf behowls the moon,
> Whilst the heavy ploughman snores,
>   All with weary task foredone.
> Now the wasted brands do glow,
>   Whilst the screech-owl, screeching loud,
> Puts the wretch that lies in woe
>   In remembrance of a shroud.
> Now it is the time of night
>   That the graves, all gaping wide,
> Every one lets forth his sprite
>   In the church-way paths to glide.
> And we fairies, that do run
>   By the triple Hecate's team
> From the presence of the sun,
>   Following darkness like a dream,
> Now are frolic; not a mouse

Shall disturb this hallowed house.
I am sent with broom before
To sweep the dust behind the door.

The children should be familiar with Puck by now. They've been merry wanderers of the night, stalkers; they've lead Bottom around and about, and been Oberon's servant making a girdle round the earth. Now it is time to stand before the curtains as they slowly close, or as the stage lighting darkens, and to write farewell poems for their versions of Puck's story. If your children have played with the lessons so far in this book, all this lesson needs is a sensitive reading of Puck's farewell lines.

Read them a few times to yourself, aloud, to get the music. All those long vowel noises, for example – 'roars', 'behowls', 'snores', 'shroud' and others might be said slowly. With other words, you might emphasise the eeriness: 'screech-owl', 'screeching', 'shroud' again, 'wretch' and 'graves'. A few of the words need explaining: 'brand' is 'torch'; 'shroud' is the cloth that covers a corpse; Hecate was a Greek goddess who presided over witchcraft.

Here are some eight- and nine-year-olds writing while in the grip of these lines:

As darkness creeps into view,
The snorzes and grunts
Of sleepers fill the night air.
The TVs die,
The babies stop their crying
For the break of night comes.
The streets are left bare
All but an alley cat
That scavenges in the bins.
This sorrow is farewell to today
But welcome to dark cold nights
For I am left to clear away

The light of day
And give to earth
The gift of night.

Rachael

I accept 'snorzes' as her own creative invention, a mix of 'snooze' and 'snores', and I see 'break of night' for what it is: a cliché ('break of day' is obviously in her mind) that she has rinsed clean, a little luckily, perhaps, for subtle re-use.

Now midnight falls, the sun sinks to sleep,
the world is empty with a lonely atmosphere.
Throughout the daylight, the silver
moon was always going to interrupt.
The air is filled with overnight
invaders who make their own space
here in the darkened creepy alley
snoring, snoring, snoring.

Charlotte

Lesson Ten: Designing Puck's costume – An art lesson

This is one of several art lessons in this book. They are all based on the same premise.

Ask the children to pretend that they are in charge of the wardrobe department, and that the producer of a modern-day dress production of *A Midsummer Night's Dream* has asked them to design a costume for Puck. What he wears has to tell the audience something about his behaviour and character even before, at the beginning of 2:1, he has opened his mouth.

Say: 'Imagine a pause before he talks to the Fairy ('I am that merry wanderer') and draw Puck as he does something that you know by now is just like him. What will he wear?' Or they might imagine him stalking Bottom, or dropping the potion into someone's eyes, or sprinting, or flying, round the globe. Or they might draw him as he watches the spirits gliding in the church paths, or as he sweeps the dust behind the door.

Ask them to make notes on their drawings to give further assistance to the producer.

Once the children have studied other characters in the play, the same teaching leads to the drawing of costumes for Bottom, Titania and the lovers.

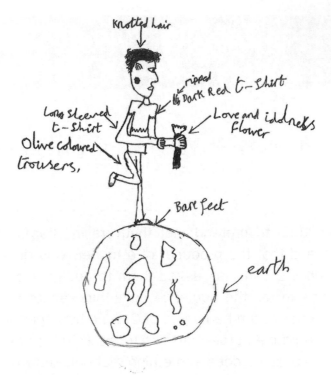

Figure 2.1 Puck running back to Oberon, by Ayesha

3 'I am such a tender ass'
Bottom and Company

First, a note about the name. The word 'bottom' did not arrive at the meaning 'buttocks', 'bum', 'posterior', or (if you speak American English) 'ass' until 1794 – nearly two hundred years after Shakespeare's death (see the *Shorter Oxford English Dictionary*). And the word 'ass' here has purely animal connotations (big ears, big everything else). Nevertheless Bottom is an appropriate name for this character: it denotes a ball on which thread is wound, and Bottom is a weaver.

He arrives at the beginning of 1:2, a scene that dispels, with a raucous humour, all that adolescent frothing about love the young people have indulged in. Within a page of Shakespeare's script we know a great deal about this man. He misuses words, he constantly interrupts, he gets in the way, he overacts and – this will prove useful for our young writers (because every writer has to go through the experience of overdoing words as Bottom overdoes his acting) – he has a relish for over-the-top verse: 'The raging rocks / And shivering shocks / Shall break the locks / Of prison gates . . .' – verse that Peter Quince, we assume, has written for him. Bottom has big ears and a big voice and, at least on the face of it, a big ego; though, as the children will discover, he can also be vulnerable. And he can be wise, too, especially on the subject of love.

Like most lower class characters in Shakespeare's plays, he speaks in prose (except for the lines in the play within the play, which are bad verse, or doggerel, not poetry – more of which later). To demonstrate the difference between 'posh' verse in the play and the prose speech of the lower classes, the children might contrast Bottom's conversation with Quince in 1.2 with the opening of 1.1, with its formal conversation between Theseus and Hippolyta.

Bottom is a labourer with ordinary aims and desires; he's not bright. He's bombastic and boastful – he implies he knows the play they are about to rehearse, but he is deceiving himself – he doesn't even know who Pyramus is. But (this will emerge later) he is a decent man. In 4.2 his friends tell us how they see him: 'sweet bully Bottom . . . the best wit of any handicraft man in Athens'. He is a gentle sceptic, utterly unsentimental, and a perfect foil for the fooled, potion-sozzled Titania: 'to say the truth, reason and love keep little company together nowadays' he tells her. And he is brave. To sum him up: as Bloom writes (1999) 'there is no darkness in [him]'.

Lesson Eleven: Playing Pyramus

Here are some of Bottom's lines from 1.2. Where the dots are, other characters speak . . . or are trying to:

> You were best to call them all generally, man by man, according to the scrip . . . good Peter Quince, say what the play treats on; then read the names of the actors; and so grow to a point . . . Now, good Peter Quince, call forth your actors by the scroll. Masters, spread yourselves . . . Name what part I am ready for, and proceed . . . What is Pyramus? A lover or a tyrant? . . . I will ask some tears in the true performing of it . . . I will move storms . . . let me play Thisbe too . . .

Read the lines quoted above. They are orders, mostly: 'You were best to . . .', 'say . . .', 'read . . .', 'grow to a point . . .', 'Masters, spread yourselves'. Or else they are boasts: 'I will ask some tears . . .', 'I will move storms'. Convey an alpha male feel in your reading, bossy, arrogant. Travel round the room, issuing the lines as demands on individuals.

Then ask the children to think of adjectives and phrases that would apply to Bottom, and write up what they offer. When the class has run out of ideas, suggest that each of them use a thesaurus, looking up some of the words you've written up to see what other words emerge.

Here are some words that children in a class offered:

awkward, bossy, loud, dominating, naggy, big-headed, conceited, wanting to be the centre of everything, silly, confused, clog-brained, arrogant, cocky, daft, boastful, self-centred, an interrupter . . .

Lesson Twelve: I will, I will, let me!

Here is Bottom in 1.2 again at ll.20–23. Bottom isn't just bossy, he is boastful too.

. . . That will ask some tears in the true performing of it. If I do it, let the audience look to their eyes: I will move storms, I will condole, in some measure. To the rest – yet my chief humour is for a tyrant. I could play Ercles rarely, or a part to tear a cat in, to make all split . . .

> Every child has strong feelings about braggartly classmates. Ask them to write a poem with lines beginning with Bottom's phrases 'I will . . . I could . . .', and finish each line with a boast. You might add some others, 'I can . . .' and (so that their poem can contain boasts about past deeds) 'I have . . .' You could quote Glendower's boast from *Henry IV Part One*: 'I can call spirits from the vasty deep' (3.1.50).

I will dance all my way to winning Strictly.
I will discover new planets in other solar systems.
Let me sing to you and I will make you fall in love with the sound of my voice.
I can write the poem that will make Shakespeare laugh.
I can make the Halloween creatures kind.

Samuel

Lesson Thirteen: Rehearsing most obscenely

Bottom gets words wrong: he uses malapropisms before that word existed. It comes from the French *mal a propos,* 'not to the purpose', and was invented by R. B. Sheridan for his play *The Rivals* as a name for the character Mrs Malaprop, who talks like this: 'She's as headstrong as an *allegory* on the banks of the Nile' . . . '*illiterate* him . . . quite from your memory' . . . 'I have done everything in my power since I *exploded* the affair'. Tell the children this. Most will readily understand the first of this trio: she meant, of course, 'alligator'. The others will have to be explained: 'obliterate' and 'exposed'. Here are some of Bottom's malapropisms:

1.2.2   generally (?singly)

1.2.43   monstrous (this is not a pure malapropism, as 'monstrous' is not necessarily about size; but it works as one)

1.2.66   aggravate (?lessen)

1.2.85   obscenely (what can he mean here?)

3.1.25   wildfowl (used with 'lion')

3.1.66   odious for odorous

4.1.35   exposition for (disposition to)

Read them to the children. Point out that there are still Mrs Malaprops and Bottoms around today. A travel agent suggested that I caught a Eurostar train from 'St Pancreas', and I have often heard 'muriel' for 'mural' (an invention, I am told, by a character in the soap opera *Coronation Street*). A football manager was quoted in a newspaper saying that 'everyone expects footballers to be confident, vicarious ('vivacious' perhaps?) creatures' when in fact, 'they are a pretty insecure bunch'. My friend was more than slightly troubled when a nurse referred to his 'prostrate'.

After discussing some of these, ask the children to think up their own malapropisms.

I did this with my apprentices. They came up with the following, some more plausible than others, but all evidence of that important need to play with language, a need anyone who wants to write well must have. Good dictionaries helped:

I have a paroxysm for music. (passion)
You look very elephant in that new dress.
I am having a taboo done on my arm tomorrow.
A figure with two opposite sides equal is called a rhinoceros.
Is there too much dalek in this soup?
I am interested in all things hysterical. (historical)
The pilot came down safely in his parasite.

The children might discuss malapropisms at home, and bring examples their parents suggest, either real ones, or made up ones.

Lesson Fourteen: Thou art translated! – Another drama lesson

Shakespeare's influence on children's writing has been my main interest so far, and it still is. But children in schools should explore Shakespeare's words in actions as well as in writing, and in all of these passages from the plays there are opportunities for drama inside the classroom or, preferably, in the school hall or the gym. What follows is an opportunity for children to play with the script and with each other, and thereby to learn about it. And to learn about each other, of course: drama is social education. This could be produced in groups of six, either as a radio play, or with actions. It's more than a lesson; it's a project that could stretch out over some days.

You will need copies of this section of the play.

Here, at 3.1.75–107, the workmen are rehearsing. Then Bottom is changed into an ass by Puck. It all begins with Flute's words (as Thisbe in the play within the play) 'Most radiant Pyramus', and climaxes at Titania's famous line 'What angel wakes me from my flowery bed'.

The sequence has 12 speeches in 32 lines. This means that everyone in the group can have a go at acting – but note that everyone should have a chance to be Bottom or Puck. Not a word of it is too hard for children, and 'brisky' is not really obscure – the children should mentally just drop the 'y'. 'Juvenal' (a Shakespearean invention from the Latin) is a joke word for 'young man'.

The lines are staccato in movement and full of action. It is funny – and suddenly at one point intensely sad: the moment when Bottom stands alone and tries to convince himself, by singing his song about the male blackbird ('ousel cock'), that he is brave. Children will recognise Bottom's feelings from remembered moments when they have been, or felt they were, alone on the playground. Titania hears him singing, wakes, and says that one line which should always raise a laugh.

Discuss all this with the children, and ask them to take turns with different parts to produce the scene. These are some questions for the children to bear in mind:

- How can we make Quince's exasperation at l. 80 onwards funny? What will we do at each exclamation mark in l.86 ('O monstrous! . . . ')?

- How will he express his fear at Bottom's appearance in this line? A great contrast with l.80 is needed here.

- How will Puck speak his stalking lines? Quickly, menacingly, teasingly? Children should collect other adverbs and discuss which ones suit the words Puck is speaking here.

- How will the other mechanicals react during the time they are on stage, especially at the point where they do not have any lines? Point out that good acting is often seen in reacting to other characters.

- How can we make Bottom look terribly alone at l.99 onwards as he talks to himself, and how will he sing his donkey-song?

- And, finally, how can we make Titania sound truly in love at l.107? Here we need another contrast: a donkey singing, and a beautifully-spoken queen (or could she be spoken in a different way?) falling instantly in love with him.

Once the children are familiar with the scene, ask them to work in groups discussing those questions (and any others they think of) for twenty minutes, with one of them making notes. They should make notes about the way they think the scene should be presented.

Here are some notes made by my apprentices printed in *italics* in the script:

FLUTE (as Thisbe) Most radiant Pyramus, most lilywhite of hue,
Of colour like the red rose on triumphant briar,
Most brisky juvenal, and eke most lovely Jew,
As true a tyrant horse that yet would never tire,
I'll meet thee, Pyramus, at Ninny's tomb

Flute speaks very squeaky but clear, like his name. He speaks slowly, he cannot always remember his lines. He finds 'triumphant' difficult to say.

QUINCE

His face is red with anger. He grits his teeth like he's having a tantrum. He shouts

'Ninus' tomb', man!

waving his arms in the air at Flute. But he calms down —

why, you must not speak that yet; that you answer to Pyramus . . .

FLUTE O — *In his normal voice, stupid-sounding*
(as Thisbe) *High voice again*

As true as truest horse, that yet would never tire.

Enter Puck, and Bottom with an ass's head on

Puck follows Bottom with a fancy jog. Sometimes behind Bottom, sometimes in front of him, sometimes beside him. Bottom walks on slowly and speaks in a big loud country voice. He thinks he is a brilliant actor!

BOTTOM (as Pyramus) If I were fair, fair Thisbe, I were only thine.

He speaks like a pirate, in a country accent

QUINCE O monstrous! O strange! We are haunted! Pray, masters, fly, masters! Help!

He whispers the first sentence in horror, gets louder and screams the last one. He is desperate for help. He looks around him in case there's anyone who can help. The others disappear to the edges of the stage and stand looking, hardly daring to. Puck speaks very quickly, like he does everything very quickly:

PUCK I'll follow you: I'll lead you about a round,
    Through bog, through bush, through brake, through briar;
Sometime a horse I'll be, sometime a hound,
    A hog, a headless bear, sometime a fire,

And neigh, and bark, and grunt, and roar, and burn
Like horse, hound, hog, bear, fire at every turn.

Puck says these words as fast as he can, but with short breaks at each comma. He turns his whole body from side to side after each line, making his eyes stare in different directions as if he is following someone.

BOTTOM Why do they run away? This is a knavery of them to make me afeard.

Enter SNOUT very nervous.

SNOUT O Bottom, thou art changed. What do I see on thee?

Confused look while scratching head. He whimpers at the end.

BOTTOM What do you see? You see an ass head of your own, do you?

Laughs at his joke.,

(Exit SNOUT)

QUINCE Bless thee, Bottom, bless thee! Thou art translated!

He is horrified, wimpy, shocked.

BOTTOM I see their knavery. This is to make an ass of me, to fright me, if they could; but I will not stir from this place, do what they can. I will walk up and down here, and will sing, that they shall hear I am not afraid.

Bottom acts royal and waves his arms about. Sometimes he chews his nail. He sings out of tune.

The ousel cock so black of hue,
With tawny-orange bill,
The throstle with his note so true,
The wren with little quill

TITANIA (waking) What angel wakes me from my flowery bed?

Rubs her eyes. She pauses after 'angel'. She stares at Bottom. Like in a trance.

Subsequently, we might put this on with these actions and others. Further questions to ask the children are:

- How will Flute move as he describes his love for Pyramus?
- How can we make Bottom look terribly alone, and how will he sing his donkey-song?
- How do they react to Puck? Can they see him? Hear him?
- What props do the actors carry? In particular, what does the actor playing Quince need?
- How are we going to give the impression that Bottom has become a donkey?
- Finally, children who have got to know the play really well – made it theirs – might ask themselves the question 'How are we going to act bad acting well?'

There are other passages in the play that can be treated in this way. One is 1:2.171, where Bottom and the others meet for casting. With this passage the children should be asked to read the words three times: once silently, then aloud, and then in pairs. They should ask themselves questions such as:

- What do you know about each character? Make a list of adjectives for each of them.

- What do their names tell you?

- Bottom butts in all the time. How can they make each interruption funny?

- Quince tends to contradict himself, producing oxymorons. Find them.

Finally, once the characters are well known to the children, they might put on a voice-only version of all or parts of 5:1:166 ('O grim-looked night') up to line 319 ('Adieu, adieu, adieu!').

Lesson Fifteen: It shall be called 'Bottom's dream' because it hath no bottom

Next, Bottom is himself again, woken, he supposes from a dream (4.1. 200–207):

> I have had a most rare vision. I have had a dream, past the wit of man to say what dream it was. Man is but an ass if he go about to expound this dream. Methought I was – there is no man can tell what. Methought I was – and methought I had – man is but a patched fool if he will offer to say what I had. The eye of man hath not heard, the ear of man hath not seen, man's hand is not able to taste, his tongue to conceive, nor his heart to report what my dream was!

Two points: 'Man is but an ass' is a perfect example of dramatic irony: the audience knows something that Bottom doesn't – that he has, indeed, been an ass himself. And also, the last sentence is a travesty of a verse in the New Testament: you might read 1 Corinthians 2:9 to the children, and then repeat Bottom's speech from 'The eye of man . . .' Perhaps that great big King James Bible that was sent to every school a few years ago has some brief use here?

> Read those lines to the children in a confused, just-woken-up-not-sure-where-I-am sort of voice. Pause for thought at every full stop and every dash, and mime puzzled thinking like a stage dimwit: screw your face up as if in a massive intellectual struggle, scratch your head, gaze up to heaven as if looking for an answer, gaze sadly at the ground when it never comes. I can imagine Winnie the Pooh, that bear of very little brain, saying these lines well.
> Ask the children to write a confused speech after a strange dream.

This writer used ellipses and repetition to good effect:

> *What, what, what was that?*
> *I dreamed that, that . . . I climbed high . . .*

I climbed a thousand steps...I caught a glimpse of...
I caught a glimpse of the golden gates, the gates,
The sky, snow, no, not snow...clouds!
I dreamed I climbed high, a thousand steps...the golden gates,
No, gone! Fury burning in my heart . . .
Then I fell from a thousand steps, falling, down, down, down...
A thousand steps, falling...

Rache

Lesson Sixteen: Raging rocks, grim-looked nights, bloody, blameful blades and mantles stained with blood – Bad verse I

As soon as I started thinking about Bottom's contribution to this book, an attractive contradiction, an oxymoron, a paradox emerged: could Bottom's first verse speech, which is (intentionally on Shakespeare's part, of course) bad verse, inspire children to write well? I explained the context to some children: the Athens workmen had gathered in the forest to rehearse a play to put on before the court. Bottom demonstrates how he could play a hero. He does it with these lines:

> The raging rocks
> And shivering shocks
> Shall break the locks
> Of prison gates,
> And Phibbus' car
> Shall shine from far,
> And make and mar
> The foolish Fates.
> > 1:2:24–31

Explain that by 'Phibbus' Bottom means Phoebus, the god of the sun, and that his 'car' is the chariot that he rides across the sky during the day. Ask the children to study this speech, and then to work out the rhyme scheme. The first three lines rhyme with the sound *ocks*, the fourth and the eight with the sound *ates*, and lines five to seven rhyme with the sound *ar*: so it's *aaabcccb*. This may look like algebra, but it's not, it's much simpler.

Children often enjoy coming across this slightly recondite knowledge, useful in no other context but as a way of recording rhyme.

The children understand, or will understand in a moment, that Bottom is showing off to his fellow-actors: the joke is that the lines, which he thinks are 'lofty', are in fact the over-the-top, out-of-date lines: lines that a bad writer might think suitable for a heroic actor.

Act Bottom's lines now, speaking as exaggeratedly as you can (hamming it up, once again, much as Bottom is doing). Easy: just act badly! But not in a shy way . . . Imitate raging and shivering and breaking on the relevant words. Then discuss the lines: what is absurd about them? The children might pick up the 'raging rocks', for example: rocks at the edge of the land don't move at all, and they certainly don't 'rage'; they know that rocks will never break locks, and that the idea that the sun's carriage ('car') will affect fates is absurd. And they know that the rhyming is ludicrous.

Ask them to write an even more hammy speech. Suggest that they build a stack of haphazard rhymes up the right-hand side of their own poems (like 'rocks . . . shocks . . . locks' etc. – but they must find different ones). That is the start. Then they must build up lines across the page to each rhyme. They might also, as Bottom does, true to his character, overdo the alliteration.

Excess is the key here, excess of rhyme, alliteration, whatever.

For once, barely forgivable effects in the writing of verse – rhymes with no necessary connection, such as 'sea . . . me . . . bee'; the ugly casual and (therefore) wrong rhyme of 'turf/earth', which children often mis-hear as a true rhyme; the meaningless sequences 'boat . . . goat . . . coat' and 'boulder . . . shoulder'; the ancient pop song rhymes, 'love . . . above . . . dove'; the frequent appearances of easy English rhymes like 'say . . . away . . . stay': for once all these infelicities are legitimate. Mention some of these to the children, or think up some of your own: you can do this by simply looking out of the window, as I am about to do now: 'brick . . . click . . . Mick . . . toad . . . road . . . flowed . . . ' and so on.

These children from different schools had come together as keen writers:

The singing sea
and mighty me
shall never cry if stung by bee.

And evil spirits
will have to pass me
to destroy earth,
my turf.

                    Anna

The boasting boat
the giant goat
and the clumsy coat
will push the brilliant boulder.

The crazy cat
the brainy bat
and the mystified mat
will shake the shivering shoulder.

                    Davida

See me tackle that monster of evil
for I beat any old weevil
so do not call me a gormless medieval.

I am easily princess of noble and glory
for I will be lord of all stable seas
and keeper of keys.

                    Kate

Lesson Seventeen: Raging rocks II – A drama session

Once they are attuned to the idea of excess, ask the children to see who can produce the most overdone, exaggerated, inflated, far-fetched, hyperbolic performance of the lines beginning 'The raging rocks'. Suggest that they learn them by heart first, and then work in pairs. One student should rehearse while the other makes suggestions – effectively being the producer, director and prompt. Then they should swap roles. After a while, each pair might present its work to another pair, and then each new foursome might work with another foursome, and so on. Thus you can bring the element of audience into the work.

The next pair of lessons presents an unusual experience for children. They are about death, so the material is ripe for a tragedy. But they are, in any decent production of the play, very funny.

Lesson Eighteen: O grim-looked night – Bad verse II

With these lines, we jump to the end of the play. Quince and his actors are putting on what is called 'the play within the play'. A tragedy, *The Most Lamentable Comedy and Cruel Death of Pyramus and Thisbe*, takes place in front of the court characters in *A Midsummer Night's Dream*.

First, Bottom is Pyramus the lover addressing the wall through which he hopes to see his lady Thisbe:

> O grim-looked night, O night with hue so black,
> O night which ever art when day is not!
> O night, O night, alack, alack, alack,
> I fear my Thisbe's promise is forgot!
> And thou, O wall, O sweet and lovely wall,
> That stand'st between her father's ground and mine,
> Thou wall, O wall, O sweet and lovely wall,
> Show me thy chink, to blink through with mine eyne.
> Thanks, courteous wall; Jove shield thee well for this!
> But what see I? No Thisbe do I see.
> O wicked wall, through whom I see no bliss,
> Cursed be thy stones for thus deceiving me!
>
> 5.1.167–178

First, read these lines as melodramatically as you can. Pyramus/ Bottom is bewailing the fact that he has (as he thinks) been stood up by Thisbe. Then ask the children what are the most commonly used words. They are, of course, 'O', 'night', 'alack' and 'wall'. Suggest that they might write some lines beginning with 'O grim-looked night', repeating certain words.

These examples come from a mixed-ability class:

O grim-looked night that is a prison!
A prison cell, a prison, prison, prison!
A grim cell, where I am locked,
Locked, locked in the grim dark!

Jack

Another example of terrible verse from the same class:

Night night night where never will be day.
A day day day which never shall be night.
A dark dark dark which ever shall be bright
A bright bright bright which never shall be light.
Show me o tree I will not never see.
That tree is me that me is tree.

Jeremy

Lesson Nineteen: O dainty duck.
O dear! – Bad verse III

And here is Bottom again as he discovers Thisbe dead (again, as he assumes) at 5.1.260–276:

> But stay – O spite!
> But mark, poor Knight,
> What dreadful dole is here
> Eyes, do you see?
> How can it be?
> O dainty duck. O dear!
> Thy mantle good –
> What, stained with blood?
> Approach, ye furies fell!
> O Fates, come, come,
> Cut thread and thrum,
> Quail, crush, conclude, and quell.
>
> 5.1.260–271

There is no need to explain the few obscure words. The meanings of 'courteous', 'bliss', 'dole', 'mantle', can be inferred from the context – and if they can't, does it matter so much? And the manic alliteration, and the bad rhymes – all of this is obvious, and so is the fact that these passages speak much more of Bottom's character than they do of Pyramus' grief. It is not difficult for children to imitate.

Ask them to do just that – to write a truly bad poem, with bad rhymes and loads of alliteration that mourns a death.

This next writer is responding, not to these lines, but to very similar ones spoken by Flute, acting Thisbe, when she discovers the genuinely dead Pyramus at 5.1.306–329. The children should bear in mind that they are especially absurd because the actor whose character is being portrayed here is Bottom, hardly a 'dove' with 'lily lips':

> Asleep, my love?
> What, dead, my dove?
> O Pyramus, arise.
> Speak, speak! Quite dumb?
> Dead, dead? A tomb
> Must cover thy sweet eyes.
> These lily lips,
> This cherry nose,
> These yellow cowslip cheeks
> Are gone, are gone . . .

In Ayesha's writing, I enjoyed the collisions of 'dear / pier', 'mourn / lawn' and 'cloudy / rowdy': I had told the children that rhyme should always serve a purpose in the making of the meaning of a poem; here, it doesn't:

> Oh dear
> My lovely
> You were my pier.
> I have talked to the ocean.
> O sisters, brothers, come to mourn
> My lover who has died on my lawn.
> Now skies turn cloudy.
> Things will get rowdy
> Make it rain, soothe his pain.
> Now I will go and cry
> Now my lover's died.
>
> Ayesha

Another example of deliberate bad writing leading to good children's writing is in the exaggerated alliteration that Peter Quince uses in his prologue at 5.1.145:

> Whereat with blade, with bloody, blameful blade,
> He bravely broached his boiling bloody breast.
> And Thisbe, tarrying in mulberry shade,
> His dagger drew, and died . . .

> Say these lines, emphasising the alliterative *bl* and *d* sounds and the melodrama. Suggest that the children go for excess . . . alliteration, rhyme . . .

Some examples from children who have been encouraged to go for broke:

> O tree, o tree, o treacherous tree,
> your furled fingers reach down
> and crush my heart so soft,
> your hurtful, horrible leaves sway
> in the harsh wind,
> your rigid bark sears my face . . .
> O tree, o tree, o treacherous tree
> Why do you always have to hurt me!?
>   Evie

> O your majesty
> I'm afraid matters have increased
> The endless killing has not ceased.
> Delve deep! Danger drives! Madness makes men mad!
>   Ayesha

Those two writers have fulfilled the task; but while Evan may have been attempting bad verse, he's done something else:

> A long road trip
> the long road trip,
> the dreaded road trip.
> The grassy moors, the gusty trees.
> Oh the long road trip
> with sheep as white as paper. Is the car moving? Is it? Is it? Is it?
> The demon road trip.
> The road trip, the road trip,
> a long beat it is.
>
> *Evan*

Oh the monotony of cross country family car rides.

Lesson Twenty: Reason and love

In 3.1., Bottom, just changed into an ass, says something to Titania that I feel is the moral centre of the play, something that works against the 'musical discord' and the 'sweet thunder' that make up all the other events. When Titania proclaims, 'I love thee' at 3.1.118, Bottom replies:

Methinks, mistress, you should have little reason for that. And yet, to say the truth, reason and love keep little company together nowadays; the more the pity that some honest neighbours will not make them friends . . .

The last eight words mean that some people will not make reason and love friends. Here, 'reason' means something like 'common sense'. Discuss this with the children: which of the characters in the play have made reason and love friends? Who have been reasonable in their loving?

When the children have studied other characters in The *Dream,* they should write the names down and then a quotation from each character that tells us something about his or her attitude to love; then a sentence of their own to say to what extent that character has made reason and love friends.

For example:

Theseus (to his bride) 'I wooed thee with my sword'. I wouldn't trust anyone wooing me with a deadly weapon.

Lesson Twenty-One: More for the Wardrobe Department

> ➤ Say: 'You have been asked to design costumes for Bottom, one as he is on his first appearance at the beginning of 1:2, and one as he is when 'translated' into a donkey. Don't forget, this production will be in modern dress. Ask yourself before you begin to draw 'How old is Bottom? Is he rich or poor? Do I want him to appear as a large man or a small man? Will your Bottom appear as half-man and half-donkey? Or will he just be a donkey?'

4 'Our Lovely Lady'
Titania

Titania has a chapter to herself for two reasons. First, she paints a vivid word-picture of how discord has created the 'contagious fogs . . . the rotted green corn . . .' that is afflicting the countryside; of how that discord is responsible for 'every pelting river' that has 'overborne [its] continent' (burst its banks). The lines of 2.1.87–102 speak of how Shakespeare understood that humankind's relationship with nature was inextricable. And, of course, they have a modern ring. For the children we teach, there are connections with work in science and geography. And more importantly, to lift the matter out of school, they make connections with images we see every year of extreme weather; of tsunamis battering coasts; of fires raging through forests; of tornadoes spinning in the air; of towns photographed from the air, surrounded by water.

And, second – this is a connected reason – she shows a compassion for human beings, the 'mortals [who] want [lack] their winter cheer . . .' for whom 'No night is now with hymn or carol blessed.' (ll.101–102)

She does all this in her astonishing speech about the effects on the countryside of her estrangement from Oberon. Much of it rings in our ears today with disturbing resonance: it is hardly an exaggeration, although, of course, it is an anachronism, to say this speech is about climate change, and individuals' responsibility for it. But even more than this, it is Titania's vision of human misery that is so affecting here.

But first, a lesson that Titania and her servants offer to even the youngest of our children.

Lesson Twenty-Two: You spotted snakes

In 2.2 Titania's servants are singing her to sleep:

You spotted snakes with double tongue,
Thorny hedgehogs be not seen.
Newts and blindworms, do no wrong
Come not near our Fairy Queen.
Philomel with lullaby,
Lulla, lulla, lullaby; lulla, lulla, lullaby.

Never harm
Nor spell nor charm
Come our lovely lady nigh.
So good night with lullaby.

Weaving spiders, come not here;
Hence, you long-legged spinners hence!
Beetles black, approach not near;
Worm nor snail, do no offence.
Philomel with melody
Sing in our sweet lullaby,
Lulla, lulla, lullaby; lulla, lulla, lullaby.

Never harm
Nor spell nor charm
Come our lovely lady nigh.
So good night, with lullaby.

> Read these lines quietly in an undertone, varied with stage-whispering. Emphasise, even exaggerate, both its soporific rhythm: 'You *spotted snakes* with *double tongue* / *Thorny hedge*hogs *be not seen* . . .' and its gentle consonants, especially the *n*s, *m*s and *l*s. Emphasise, too the repetitions, especially the 'lulla, lulla' lines. Your voice should imitate the action of a rocking cradle.
>
> Ask: Who would you like to write a lullaby for? A baby brother or sister? A grandma or a granddad? A pet dog or cat? Once you've raised the question give the children a minute of silence, first to make their decision, and then to think about how they might begin the lullaby. Suggest that no-one would want to say a lullaby to someone they loved with crashing, banging, thumping sounds in it.

Here is a seven-year-old boy who has written a lullaby for himself. I have reproduced exactly what he put down (though with some spelling corrections). I remember how he held a short stub of a pencil as one might hold a Stanley knife, and how the pressure he applied indented the page under the one he was writing on. His pace was, unsurprisingly, slow, and I looked over his shoulder frequently on my tour around the classroom. His concentration was total:

Harowing raptor
Oh harowing raptor gulp please don't come near me with your
shiny snapping juicy teeth and your sharp claws Oh you make me
so frightened that I run away very fast.

Harowing sharks
Oh harowing sharks please don't come near me in the sea with
your sharp puffing teeth or I will get very scared

Harowing cheeter
Oh harowing cheeter please dont make me climb on your back
because if you go fast you will make me sick

Tushil

I find that children as young as seven years old explore their own fears and fantasies in words. Tushil has done that here. Who knows what he is exploring? Or discovering? Or coming to provisional terms with? He has made an object that exists on paper. Reflecting on its shape and content may help him to face his fears with courage – that raptor, those sharks, that 'cheeter' and whatever those monsters represent (a secret, of course, even from him). Writing can be an immeasurably (I use that adverb with care, because we are supposed to measure everything in schooling today) bright light shining against the dark.

Sometimes when I teach very young children, teachers, teaching assistants, parents and other personnel take dictation. Everyone is welcome in my lessons as long as they can support the children.

A five-year-old dictated this to an adult:

Stay away nightmares
Stay away dinosaurs made of magnets
                                   Elizabeth

And another five-year-old dictated:

I don't want dragons to snap mummy
I don't want sharks to snap mummy
                                   Bhakti

When you teach this passage to older children, ask them to find the principal sounds in the song. They are, of course, those *l*s, backed up by other gentle noises: the *m*s and *n*s. They might like to know that the word supplying the root for the sounds in this lullaby is 'philomel', meaning 'nightingale'. Here are some nine-year-olds. The first is an example of a child reversing the colloquial word order, presumably in order to sound 'old fashioned' or 'poetic': not a practice normally to be encouraged:

Darkness must frighten you not;
may light shine down upon you
lullaby lullaby

Spiders shall harm you never;
wasps and bees must fall
whenever you are near them,
whenever you are near
lullaby lullaby

Moonlight, sunlight,
lightbulb glow,
all of these protect you,
all of these are yours:

lullaby lullaby
lullaby lullaby
lullaby lullaby

May moonlight slice through darkness,
may rays smash through the dark,
may dark evaporate at your feet

lullaby, lullaby

Thomas

Another similar piece had these lines at the end of each successive verse: 'butterflies will keep you safe . . . friends will keep you safe . . . daffodils will keep you safe . . . the only noise is your breath', thereby managing to add other 'soft' sounds to their poem: *fs*, for example, and that *th* that softens the relative hardness of *br*. It is all too easy to underestimate children's resourcefulness in their use of the sounds, as well as the meanings, of language.

All the children imitated Shakespeare's repetition to good effect:

Lullaby, lullaby, nothing can touch our queen.
She is protected forever from any wild animal,
From any weapons or enemy.

Lullaby, lullaby, nothing can touch our queen.
Not even the fiercest lions or leopards
Or the eerie howls of night.

Lullaby, lullaby, nothing can touch our queen.
We will protect her from the dangers of night and day
And watch over her as long as she lives.

Anon.

Lesson Twenty-Three: Contagious fogs – Titania and climate change I

This is a lesson, mainly, for the ablest or the keenest writers. Titania's great lines in 2.1 about the weather and climate change provide a climax to the first part of the play. At 2:1:60, Oberon and Titania meet, with his famous greeting, 'Ill met by moonlight, proud Titania!' and her response 'What, jealous Oberon?' Here is a course of love running far from smooth. We learn much about the characters' respective personalities over the next three pages of the script: Oberon is ready to swap accusations with his wife. She, on the other hand, is concerned about what is happening to the countryside following their estrangement.

> This lesson requires more preparation than most. Try to make the speech yours, to get inside it, reading it aloud several times before the lesson. I know that this is going to take time and effort, but I promise it is worth it. The Cambridge School Shakespeare edition of the play (see References) supplies excellent notes; the next paragraph offers a summary. I have found that it gives the children a scaffolding for their understanding. This summary starts at l.87, 'But with thy brawls . . .' and ends at l.113, ' . . . their wonted liveries':
>
> Because of your fighting, you have spoiled our amusement . . . so the winds, blowing uselessly, have taken 'revenge' and 'sucked up from the sea' fogs that will harm us as they touch us ('contagious'), and those fogs have fallen on the land, have made all the rivers burst their banks. Now there is nothing for the farm animals ('ox[en]') to do, and the ploughman is out of work. The unripe corn has rotted before it's ripe ('attained a beard'). The sheep have wandered and are all sick ('murrion') – the crows are eating them (are 'fatted') while they die. Where the people used to play nine-men's-morris (like draughts outdoors) the spaces they played on in the countryside are muddied over. The people are having no enjoyment ('winter cheer') and there's no singing ('no . . . hymn or carol'). The moon who rules floods is angry and people are

sick in their muscles and joints. And the seasons are mixed up. There's frost in summer and spring buds in winter (Hiems' ice. All the seasons swap their colours ('wonted liveries') with one another.

Then act the speech to children as best you can. Finally, tell them that they have an opportunity now to 'bring these lines up to date'.

. . . with thy brawls thou hast disturbed our sport.
Therefore the winds, piping to us in vain,
As in revenge have sucked up from the sea
Contagious fogs; which, falling in the land,
Hath every pelting river made so proud
That they have overborne their continents.
The ox hath therefore stretched his yoke in vain,
The ploughman lost his sweat, and the green corn
Hath rotted ere his youth attained a beard.
The fold stands empty in the drowned field,
And crows are fatted with the murrion flock.
The nine-men's-morris is filled up with mud,
And the quaint mazes in the wanton green
For lack of tread are undistinguishable.
The human mortals want their winter cheer;
No night is now with hymn or carol blessed.
Therefore the moon, the governess of floods,
Pale in her anger, washes all the air,
That rheumatic diseases do abound;
And through this distemperature we see
The seasons alter; hoary-headed frosts
Fall in the fresh lap of the crimson rose,
And on old Hiems' thin and icy crown
An odorous chaplet of sweet summer buds
Is, as in mockery, set. The spring, the summer,

The chilling autumn, angry winter, change
Their wonted liveries, and all the mazed world
By their increase now knows not which is which . . .

It is, of course, anachronistic to talk of Titania's great speech as concerning 'climate change'. Nevertheless, phrases like 'Contagious fogs . . . pelting river[s] . . . green corn hath rotted' . . . strike an (alarm?) bell in the minds of anyone who has followed the news. I collected work from a class who had studied this speech with me, but who had also done work on extreme weather conditions with their teacher. The images all round the room – tsunamis, tornadoes, waves crashing on to promenades – all contributed to their work:

The ice caps have all worn thin and melted
Putting an end to life as we know it.
The polar bears, seals, whales and penguins,
Once at separate ends of the earth
Are connected by a vast ocean.
The continents are all under water.
Where once were streets, shops and an old church
There's now an old hutch, a tarpaulin and some bins
Floating in water that should be miles away.
There used to be a huge desert
Where that water tosses old bricks
From a pyramid around, and a sphinx too.
The Amazon rain forest is as wet as it will ever be
Though none of the animals' trees
Will keep them dry – they're washed away anyway.
Mowgli will never swing through the trees again.
Harriet

It is a curse, the animals have died.
No joy is to be seen in this world, only corpses.
Dreams of a cheerful future are shattered.

The rain has turned to dust.
Sand dominates the land.
                    Alicia

Winds, furious, attack the snow,
frost so cold it chases out the leaves,
ice ends all movement in the rivers.
Animals hide away, hiding in the warmth.
Green, red, gold and white.
Spirits and bells, old tales and gifts,
fish so cold as they swim to the bottom,
birds so warm as they take flight to the sky.
Let the winter spirit linger…
                    Luke

The dry grass turns a stale yellow colour
Smooth brown conkers flood the land beneath
The horse chestnut tree.

The strong evening light appears earlier
the first golden leaf drifts down from the tree
and the apples are ready to pick
the silky petals disconnect from the centre of the flower
beautiful stripy spiders spin their silky webs…
                    Hattie

Line 3 in this next piece reminded me of Edward Lear:

Though clocks say two down, the moon says seven night.
When tide is to be high, it is now low.
Bananas no more, instead wee green things.
Christmas in summer, Easter in autumn.

Longest day is only five hours' light.
Shortest day is fourteen hours' light.
Salt water to be found in all rivers.
Milk from pigs, sausages from goats and cows.
Eleanor

One writer began 'The winds are translated from gentle to rough', and I appreciated the way she had remembered Peter Quince's use of that verb: 'Bless thee, Bottom, bless thee! Thou art translated!' (3.1.98).

Lesson Twenty-Four: Contagious fogs – Titania and climate change II

Another way of teaching this speech is to break it down into short passages for groups of two and three to discuss. Then ask them to write down their ideas about what Titania meant by each extract. The findings can be shared with the whole class. Doing it this way would arguably be more educational than offering them a paraphrase, as I have suggested above. It depends on the children, and your confidence in them.

Lesson Twenty-Five: Contagious fogs – Titania and climate change III – An art lesson

This lesson will make a point about the relevance of Shakespeare's words to today's climatic predicament with some force. You need to surround the children with images of extreme weather from newspapers, magazines and the Internet. Scenes of flooding, especially rivers bursting their banks, landscape in hurricanes and under heavy snow, crops rotting, starving live-stock, woodland mud and so on are to be readily found. Children might paint part of the scene that Titania describes, or the one that they have written about in Lesson Twenty-Three. They should print either a line from Titania's speech, or from their own writing as a caption to their artwork.

Teaching this great speech is a challenge, but it is is a rewarding one. It brings into play some great poetry, some relevance to what is happening today all over the world, and has a powerful moral dimension in that Titania accepts some of the responsibility for the unhappiness of human beings.

5 True love? 'Two lovely berries moulded on one stem'

I don't think there's much love in The *Dream*. Theseus and Hippolyta? Lysander and Hermia? Demetrius and Helena? Swap the last four around in almost any permutation. And Oberon and Titania? And Titania and Bottom? Bottom himself has got it right, at least in this world of 'musical discord' and 'sweet thunder': 'reason and company keep little company together'.

There's no certainty about any of these relationships. One of them began in warfare, another topples in a row about a little slave boy, two others are ready to be shifted on the sands of magic, and the last one is barely a love at all, as Bottom knows full well, even if Titania doesn't. For more on loving and doting in this play, see my note in Note E.

But there is a depiction of the real love, though, and another of the unreal kind, and this chapter is based on those two.

Lesson Twenty-Six: We grew together

What about love between friends? We are on surer ground here than we are talking about adolescent and mature love. This is a love children do experience, of course, though they don't, probably, use the word – they would be embarrassed by it. It's the love that all teachers see in many of their ten-year-olds: children who have been playing together with a tennis ball or a football since they were six, others who first met in the home corner in the nursery.

Helena and Hermia have been close since they were infants and toddlers. Read the children these lines from Helena's speech from 3.2.208–214. During the row in the midsummer night's forest, Puck's potion and the men's behaviour have put them at loggerheads, and Helena, trying to heal the breach, reminds Hermia of their childhood spent together:

. . . we grew together
Like to a double cherry, seeming parted,
But yet an union in partition,
Two lovely berries moulded on one stem,
So with two seeming bodies but one heart,
Two of the first, like coats in heraldry
. . . crowned with one crest . . .

This is a powerful lesson in Personal and Social Education: the children (one hopes) will leave the classroom understanding friendship better. Ask them to close their eyes and think about a close relationship: when did it begin? Where were they? Remind them of Helena's lines about the 'double cherry' and the 'berries moulded on one stem'. Prompt them by suggesting areas of their experience which might supply similes.

These children are eight-year-olds. Each child's writing begins with 'We are like. . . .' which I had written up:

. . . *two jammy dodgers stuck together.*
                              Georgina

. . . *lego pieces building up our friendship,*
. . . *two yellow lines letting no one park on our friendship.*
                              Jamie

. . . *two paths that go the same way*
Or ear-rings in the same ear.
                              Molly

. . . *stones with our names written on them,*
like owls flapping our wings at the same pace.
Before you came along I was like a feather lying on its own
And then you gracefully floated down beside me.
                              Leah

Lesson Twenty-Seven: The course of true love?

When I studied this play at school, I soon found out that it was important to distinguish between the two young women and to have in mind the course of their 'true loves'. The children should lodge in their minds that Helena is a 'maypole' (Hermia insults her so at line 296) and that Hermia is a 'puppet' (Helena at line 288). Here is an activity for getting a grip on the love story.

> Ask the children, once they know the play a little, to look through it, reading only the words of the four young people. As they do, they should make notes: who loves whom at each point? They should add quotations to back up what they are writing, and their own comments. They should share their findings with each other.

Here's an example of how they might begin:

1.1 Lysander and Hermia (she's the smaller girl) love each other. Demetrius loves Hermia, too. No-one loves Helena (the tall one). Poor Helena. But she loves Demetrius. See II.192–193, where she says to Hermia 'O teach me how you look, and with what art / You sway the motion of Demetrius' heart'.

2.1 Demetrius hates Helena. I.212: 'For I am sick when I do look on thee'.

They will discover that the turning point is in the third act: Puck drops the potion into Lysander's eyes in 3:2, and Lysander has woken in the forest. He used to love Hermia, the little one, of course. Refer back to the beginning of the play, 1:1:128–180, where he swears that he will love her, and where he makes plans for them to run away together. But now he wakes. He sees not Hermia, the minimus, but Helena, the maypole.

Men are, indeed, as Balthazar sings in *Much Ado About Nothing* (2.2.50) 'To one thing constant never'. Or so it seems. And (as Lysander has said to Hermia) 'the course of true love never did run smooth'. There are other lessons in these lines: both provide debating points for the classroom.

Lesson Twenty-Eight: O Helen, goddess, nymph, perfect, divine!

I've suggested that the love of school friends is genuine. Now we are back to the phony love, what we might call the 'potion love'. If you know the class well, it is possible to have some fun with these lines. In 3.2, Demetrius wakes up and sees Helena, whom he has previously scorned. But through the agency of Puck, he has changed. And he proclaims in ll.137–144:

> O Helen, goddess, nymph, perfect, divine!
> To what, my love, shall I compare thine eyne?
> Crystal is muddy! O, how ripe in show
> Thy lips, those kissing cherries, tempting grow!
> That pure congealed white, high Taurus snow,
> Fanned with the eastern wind, turns to a crow
> When thou hold'st up thy hand. O let me kiss
> This princess of pure white, this soul of bliss!

Say these lines. Do it in a wildly over-cooked way, paying attention to the punctuation with, perhaps, long wondering gaps (or gasps?) at every comma, and a verbal climax at the exclamation mark. Try to convey a growing doting and phony wonder at every line. Exaggerate those ludicrous similes and images: the muddy crystal; the kissing cherries; the snow like a crow's feathers. In short, your performance should make the children laugh.

Briefly gloss 'Taurus' (a range of Turkish mountains), 'nymph', and 'eyne'. This last is worth noting. It was then an already archaic word for 'eyes', and Shakespeare is mocking an old-fashioned way, firstly of writing, and secondly of viewing women. According to a convention which in Shakespeare's time was already becoming stale, women of the court were supposed to be as pale as snow and with lips of coral red (see his wonderful mockery of it all in

Sonnet 130, a hymn not only to a real black-haired, dark-skinned woman, but to honesty).

Discuss with the children:

● Can you remember some of the comparisons made about Helena?

● How do these words sound to you?

● How would you feel if someone addressed you in this way? Especially if it were someone whom you knew was in love with someone else, which is the case here?

Think of some adjectives that describe this manner of speaking to a lover. (You could prompt them with 'exaggerated', 'pretending', and 'over-the-top' – a thesaurus will be helpful here.)

Now ask the children to write their own outrageous, insincere love poems – and then to write a response, a direct, honest put-down. As always, emphasise that their lines must not steal any of Shakespeare's. In some classes it would be helpful to have a discussion of current popular music, even to ask the class to bring examples in, and then to compare the language with Demetrius' speech. There are examples around – I hear them in the gym – but I am not mentioning them here because they would be out of date before the book is published.

You are my wish
that just
came true
and my book
full of secrets.
You're
my favourite spreading
in a sandwich
as well as
my princess

in a wedding dress.
You are
my favourite poem
in my diary
and a maths test
getting 10 out of 10
every time.
You are my hero
saving me from
a bully.

Response

All you want
Is to break me!
Hurt me!
Annoy me!
You're not the person
I thought you were,
you are just a big lump of trash
being thrown
into a river.
I knew it!

                    Rebecca

Your eyes shine so brightly they make diamonds look muddy.
You and I are a better pair than any mum or dad
You make me feel more magical than any wizard.
Your skin is like a fresh snowfall which no-one has stood on.
You're smarter than any of the inventors.
You're sweeter that 1000 kilograms of dolly mixtures.
You're a dream but in real life.
Whenever you're around it smells like freshly baked cakes.

Response
How dare you do this.
You stupid boy.
Can't you be mean and ignore me as usual?
Just go to your house and forget this ever happened.
                                                    James

Lesson Twenty-Nine: By heart

Any great poetry learnt when young is likely to be a pleasure later on in life. It should not be rote learning, forced on the children: that has the opposite effect, as many older teachers will know from their own experiences. (Learn this speech by Friday or you'll be in detention!) Learning by heart is a different matter. We simply encourage children to find some lines that appeal to them, and to learn them.

Someone looking over my shoulder has asked just, 'What is the benefit for the children to learn the lines by heart?'

First, there's a pleasure in the here and now of saying a poem on your way home from school; of muttering one in bed as you get close to sleep. Just as many children enjoy practicing kicking an oval ball high between posts, or trying to bend a round one in the way their favourite footballer does, or working on scales on a piano, or waiting by the river bank for ages and ages till they get a bite . . . just as many children enjoy these activities, many children enjoy the opportunity to learn poetry by heart. We hear less about them, because the activity of getting a poem by heart is less photogenic and potentially far, far less media-friendly than the ones I've listed above.

Second, while the ability to kick a ball hard and accurately will desert children sooner or later as strength and skill fade, a poem learnt by heart will stay with them, unless they are very unlucky in old age, for the rest of their lives. Interestingly, the ability to learn new poems declines at maturity – another reason for trying to do so in one's childhood.

More practically, children learning Shakespeare's poetry in primary school will be better prepared for studying it later at secondary school and university. I asked some nine- and ten-year-olds to learn groups of lines, and asked them to write about what they thought about the experience:

I am a singer, so I learn songs every day. I am also an actor and dancer so learning things by heart benefits me. It feels like a massive accomplishment when you've learnt something . . .

Ayesha

. . . It is often quite hard when [you're] forced but it often comes naturally, like on the radio I often start singing after only a couple of listens, and the same with Christmas carols. I think there is a benefit about learning by heart because otherwise we wouldn't be able to sing along to the radio . . .

Ellie

My experience of learning off by heart is interesting and fun because I repeat the lines in my head and think about how they sound and their meaning . . .

Evie

Ask the children to choose one character from the play, and then to choose some of that character's lines and see if they can get them by heart. Two or three lines might be enough for some; others will be able to manage more.

Here are some suggestions from the characters mentioned in this chapter:

- Any group of four or five lines from Titania's speech 'But with thy brawls' at 2.1.86–117 (see Lesson Twenty-Three).

- Oberon's lines to Puck at 2.1.249–52:

  I know a bank where the wild rhyme blows,
  Where oxlips and the nodding violet grows,
  Quite overcanopied with luscious woodbine,
  With sweet musk-roses, and with eglantine . . .

- The fairies' lullaby at the beginning of 2.2 (see Lesson Twenty-Two)

- Some of the fairies' words to Puck at the beginning of 2.1

  Over hill, over dale,
  Thorough bush, thorough briar,

Over park over pale,
Thorough flood, thorough fire;
I do wander everywhere
Swifter than the moon's sphere;
And I serve the Fairy Queen,
To dew her orbs upon the green . . .

You Taught Me Language: The Tempest

A summary

There are two groups of characters in this play: the islanders and the shipwrecked royal court. In the first group, the main character is Prospero, a magician who is responsible for the storm, and who years ago was usurped of his rightful role as Duke of Milan, and put out to sea in a boat with his baby daughter. Miranda is now a young woman. They arrived on this island. Also on the island is the monstrous Caliban, Prospero's slave, and the spirit Ariel, who is also a slave to Prospero, and who will be freed at the end of the play.

The other group is the royal court of Naples: the king, Alonso, his son, Ferdinand (who will fall in love with Miranda) and some councillors, including the kindly Gonzalo, who had been generous to Prospero and Miranda all those years ago; there's also Antonio, who has taken Prospero's place in Milan, and his wicked companion Sebastian. Having purloined a barrel of wine from the ship, the king's butler and jester, Stephano and Trinculo, provide light relief with Caliban.

The play begins with a storm, and the second group of characters are shipwrecked on the island. The king and his son mourn each other . . .

Part 2, You Taught Me Language, contains lessons which focus mainly, but not exclusively, on two characters: Caliban and Ariel, both of whom offer rich and plentiful opportunities for young children's writing.

But the lessons start with the dramatic action of the first scene. I find it hard to think of a child of eight years upwards who will not be able to write vividly with this stimulus.

6 'Boatswain!'

'One day, a long time ago, a ship with a king, his prince and all their courtiers was wrecked in a terrible storm . . .'; 'Once upon a time a noble duke and his baby daughter were pushed out to sea in a leaking boat . . .'

It is not hard to come across re-tellings of this play that begin in that bloodless way. But the first scene of *The Tempest* is all action, as vivid as a nightmare, and its power is way beyond the reach of any writer tap-tap-tapping out dreary sentences like those above.

Shakespeare's scene doesn't *tell* the tale of a storm, it *is* the storm. In your preparation, try reading it aloud and listening to the sounds your voice is making. You can hear the storm's noises in words like 'roarers', 'drowning', 'howling', 'louder', 'bawling', even 'whorson'. Towards the end, you can hear the ship's timbers creaking in all those *i*s, *t*s and *k*s. And among all that murdering row 'th'master's whistle' shrieks.

Certainly, there are a few words that children will find obscure, but we can gloss them in a moment: 'bestir', 'mariner', 'yarely' and others. But even if we don't bother, the meanings are clear from the context, and the very first speech – or roar or yell – 'Boatswain!' (pronounced 'bosun') is made up of just one word – it's a panicked attempt to clamber above the noise of the elements, like a sailor clambering up rigging – and an exclamation mark (like many a lesson, now I come to think of it: 'Quiet!', but more urgent). On stage it would be a dull production that couldn't make that frantic shout a thrill. But in the classroom too it can be dramatic.

Contributing to the drama in that opening is the contrast between the sailors' utterances – blunt, urgent, often verbless – and those of the courtiers, haughty, insulting, abusive, still largely in complete sentences despite the circumstances.

That contrast is telling, and hints at one of the play's central themes, which is authority: who has it, who has lost it, who is striving for it, how it is exercised. The first scenes in Shakespeare nearly always tell us about something critical to the play. There's a power issue at the beginning of *A Midsummer Night's Dream* as well: father versus daughter, man versus woman ('I wooed thee with my sword' says Theseus to his bride, boding ill for their marriage). And the opening of *Romeo and Juliet* is upfront about the social discord that will dominate the story. And here in *The Tempest*, society's rules are overturned. If anyone has power (though they're only just hanging on to it), it is the Master and the Boatswain: the king and his courtiers are impotent.

And all the time, hovering low over every speech, there's the growing potential of sudden death. All this is done through language, and it grips children.

Read parts of this scene, acting a shipwreck radio-wise. Use different voices for, first, the words of the sailors who are working against the storm to save themselves and, second, their royal passengers. If there is more than one adult in the room, hand out parts. The king's party are, of course, in one way or another – in their arguing, in their cursing, in their well-meant advice (Gonzalo's) – simply getting in the way. They're obstructing the sailors.

The sailors' words are printed here in Roman and the courtiers' in Italic:

Boatswain! . . . Here master. What cheer? . . . Good; speak to the mariners. Fall to yarely, or we run ourselves aground. Bestir, bestir! . . . Yare, yare. Take in the topsail. Tend to th'master's whistle [TO THE STORM] Blow till thou burst thy wind if room enough!

Good boatswain, have care. Where's the master? Play the men.

I pray now, keep below . . . Do you not hear him? You mar our labour – keep your cabins. You do assist the storm.

Nay, good, be patient.

When the sea is. Hence! What cares these roarers for the name of king? To cabin. Silence! Trouble us not.

A pox o'your throat, you bawling, blasphemous, incharitable dog . . . Hang, cur, you whorson, insolent noisemaker, we are less afraid to be drowned than thou art.

I pray now, keep below . . . You mar our labour – keep your cabins. You do assist the storm . . . Down with the topmast! Yare, lower, lower! Bring her to try with the main-course . . .

Mercy on us! We split, we split! – farewell my wife and children! Farewell, brother! We split, we split, we split! Let's all sink wi'th'king . . .

Ask the children to say some of these lines after you. Point out the curses (curses are prominent in this play). You might decide to omit 'whorson', or say it and leave it unglossed, or face up to it and explain it. Then point out the prayer ('[May God have] mercy on us!') that is heard in the confusion near the end, and the farewells.

Ask the children to imagine that they are on a ship caught in a storm at sea (or on the *Titanic,* perhaps, after the collision with the iceberg). They should close their eyes and imagine the pandemonium, the noises of the ship's timbers creaking, splitting and cracking; the furnishing rolling out of control across the decks; (or the crashing of the iceberg against the metal of the ship). They should then write their own cries.

Suggest that they might mix things up: they might thread through their writing invented swearwords, prayers, and words, or messages to cry out to family members present or absent. And some of the words might imitate the sound of the storm.

Here are two suggestions for augmenting this lesson:

First, you could surround the children as they write with images of shipwrecks – of the *Titanic,* for example. And second, you could play a recording of the fourth movement of Beethoven's Sixth Symphony. Depicting a storm, the second of the two allegros lasts three and a half minutes.

Here is a selection of some of the phrases a class of eight-year-olds wrote:

> *Have mercy! God save us! Farewell! Get outta my way! All we can do is hope and pray . . . Drag, you storm! Let us live! I wanna stay alive! Dear God send winds as soft as a touch of light. Let us live till we grow old, let us see the world and get our hope, Amen. Get outta my way! All we can do is hope and pray . . . Don't be noisy, I want to die in peace. God show mercy on us. Farewell. God save our souls. Hoist the sails! So long, wife! Must we part from our loved ones – .Tongi! Don't forget me! Jimmy, Susan, look after your mother! Noooooo! Thank you God for our lives, peace descend on us! I won't forget you! Remember good times not bad. I'm trying to pray – in peace and – Get up. God give mercy, I want to live! Forgive my sins! Somebody help! I don't wanna die!*

There is a successful mixture of ways of talking here that captures something of the panic of Shakespeare's writing: 'outta my way! . . . All we can do is hope and pray . . . Don't be noisy, I want to die in peace . . . Hoist the sails! Tongi! Don't forget me! Noooooo!' Among all the noise, one child's contribution stands out, first because of its contrast to the context, and second because of the evidence of an imagination that has created it: 'Dear God send winds as soft as a touch of light'.

All our children, given the chance, will write lines like that.

There's a drama lesson for the shipwreck scene in Note F.

Lesson Thirty-One: Die a dry death

Read Gonzalo's last words before the ship is wrecked:

> Now would I give a thousand furlongs of sea for an acre of barren ground – long heath, brown furze, anything. The wills above be done, but I would fain die a dry death.

Explain that long heath and brown furze is heather and gorse – ground that can't be farmed. Ask the children: what would they settle for to be safe from the storm – anything on dry land, however uncomfortable or humble?
This is a twelve-year-old responding to Gonzalo's speech.

Rescue me you powers of heaven from this mad sea but give me a hedge to hide in. I would give the whole Atlantic for a shop doorway to be dry in and cardboard to cover me if I could be away from this evil crashing sea and the cries of men dying. Save me powers of heaven from this evil sea, give me a little bed in a cold room as long as it is dry, you powers of heaven. As long as it is quiet.

Alison

Lesson Thirty-Two: What cares these roarers?

This is a simple way of getting a poem going.

> Ask the children to choose a line from the shipwreck scene and make it the beginning of a new poem. Each of the lines in the new poem should be roughly the same length as the Shakespeare line. I suggest one of the following as beginnings:
>
> Cheerly, cheerly, my hearts!
> Out of our way, I say.
> What cares these roarers for the name of king?
> All lost! To prayers, to prayers, all lost!
> Remember whom thou hast aboard.
> Give thanks that you have lived so long.
>
> It is an opportunity to be melodramatic, and to be free with something I usually discourage, the exclamation mark.

Here are some nine-year-olds enjoying the drama:

What cares these roarers for the name of king?
Are the seas bothered that you are prime minister?
Is the lightning impressed that you are a famous man?
In this place no-one is impressed by you or what you are,
No-one cares a tiny bit for all your importance.

Declan

Cheerly, cheerly, my hearts!
Pull the rope hard, hard, hard.
and listen for the whistle
and follow your orders now
unless you want to sleep
with the fishes tonight.
                              Jenny

Remember whom thou hast aboard.
There are great men aboard this ship,
kings, princes, councillors,
dukes and lords and their ladies
all with their importance at home
Remember whom thou hast aboard.

Remember whom thou hast aboard.
There are politicians,
people with power,
people who can do what they want when they want.
Remember whom thou hast aboard.
                              James

Out of our way, I say.
Out of our way!
Off the decks with you!
Get back to your cabins!
Or I'll throw you in the sea!
                              Ella

Give thanks that you have lived so long
give thanks for all the air you breathed
give thanks for the waters you swam in

give thanks for the hills you climbed
and ran down the other sides of
give thanks for the blue skies of summer
and the lights on a Christmas tree

Jo

7 'Be not afear'd'
Caliban

'You taught me language'. So says Caliban to Prospero in 1:2 of *The Tempest*. And Caliban, as we shall see, and as the children will understand, is a master of language. But he is, in part, a monster, and he continues: 'and my profit on't / Is, I know how to curse.' His cowardly viciousness is explored in Lessons Thirty-Six to Thirty-Eight, What I concentrate on here is how he has not only learned language: he has also learned how to use it in the most intense way. Like all poets, like Adam in Genesis, he has learned the names of things. For Adam in Genesis 2:20, it was 'all cattle, . . . the fowl of the air, and every beast of the field'; for Caliban it is 'pig-nuts', 'clust'ring filberts', 'marmosets' and 'scamels'.

Gibson, in his Cambridge edition of the play, reiterates something worth pointing out to children early in their study of Shakespeare. As a rule, high-status characters speak in verse, while comic or low-status characters speak in prose; however, the unquestionably low-status (though not comic) Caliban speaks some of Shakespeare's greatest poetry. This should warn us against seeing him as a mere brute.

This monster-poet is whatever you might choose of these: a contradiction, a paradox, a walking (or crawling – Prospero calls him a 'tortoise') oxymoron. So to learn about him, and to write under the influence of the words written for him, is to learn much about Shakespeare's method: his way with contradictory doubles. Every time I see *The Tempest* I hope to see an actor who will show us both more of the poetic side of Caliban and more of his brutality as well.

Lesson Thirty-Three: Legged like a man – and his fins like arms

But before we listen to Caliban the poet, here he is as someone else sees him. In 2.2 the jester Trinculo, just off the wrecked ship, catches sight of the terrified Caliban, who is flat out on the ground trying to hide ('Perchance he will not mind me'). Trinculo ponders:

> What have we here – a man, or a fish? Dead or alive? A fish, he smells like a fish; a very ancient and fishlike smell; a kind of, not-of-the-newest poor-John. A strange fish . . . Legged like a man – and his fins like arms. Warm, o' my troth . . . this is no fish, but an islander . . .

> 2.2.23–33 (excerpts)

Say the lines haltingly. Put long pauses at most of the punctuation marks to represent the thinking of a not-very-bright man; or of a man, perhaps, who *is* bright, but pretending to be dim: a man who is teasing Caliban, much as parents tease young children who think they have hidden themselves, while in fact a hand or a foot protrudes.

Either way, you should be able to make the lines funny: suitable gestures at the words about the fishy smells help (a 'poor-John' was a salted fish eaten mostly by the poor). If you know the children well, you might pick on one child to be your stooge, and pretend that he or she is Caliban. Or better, walk around the room picking on the children one by one.

Then ask the children to imagine coming across a creature somewhere – in a forest, on the seashore, in the street – that's hard to identify. They should write in this halting style, making sure that they employ words that use more than one of the senses. Does the creature make any noise? Perhaps they could nervously touch it – what does it feel like? Smell like? For the sake of variety, ban fishy writing: they could instead use words for scales, for fur, for rough hair, and words about heat and cold.

Here are some sentences from an eight-year-old:

It sounds like a frog that sighs. I hear it scraping its long thin fingers on the rocks. When you touch it, it burps and spits and farts. Is it a platypus? It has kangaroo breath. Is it a smelly shoe or my brother's nappy? There's a lingering stench and it's spongy and curly.

Jenny

Lesson Thirty-Four: I'll show thee the best springs

A few lines later in the same scene, Trinculo and Stephano (respectively a jester and a drunken butler who have escaped the storm) are getting to know Caliban. Here is that 'deformed slave' making them welcome to the island with his poetry at 2.2.146–147 and 153–159:

> I'll show thee the best springs; I'll pluck thee berries;
> I'll fish for thee, and get thee wood enough.
>
> . . .
>
> I prithee let me bring thee where crabs grow;
> And I with my long nails will dig thee pig-nuts,
> Show thee a jay's nest, and instruct thee how
> To snare the nimble marmoset. I'll bring thee
> To clust'ring filberts, and sometimes I'll get thee
> Young scamels from the rock . . .

Act these lines, emphasising their welcoming character: Caliban is pleased to see humans that, he supposes, will not tyrannise him as Prospero has. His repetition of 'thee' (ten times in just eight lines, and reinforced in 'prithee'), makes this almost fawning friendliness even clearer.

Once you have read the lines two or three times, give some explanations. Pig-nuts are usually acorns, though why Caliban should be interested in them is obscure; filberts are hazel nuts, and a marmoset is small monkey. What are 'scamels': gulls? Kittiwakes? Fulmars? Or godwits? The *Oxford English Dictionary* quotes Shakespeare's use here as the first recorded one, but it may be an old word for 'limpet'.

Suggest that the children think for a while of some place where they were happy, a place where they had plenty of unfamiliar, fulfilling things to do;

perhaps (but not necessarily) a place they visited on holiday. Or it could be the country of their birth. They should write lines to a friend inviting him or her to stay with them. Give the children a minute or two of silence with their eyes closed so that they can remember the place, and then ponder their memories. Jog them into thinking in terms of all five senses. And then, still in that blind silence (in which, paradoxically, their memories *are* seeing) they should put their memories into the shapes of sentences.

Then ask them if anyone would like to share a memory with the rest of the class. After listening to one or two, get them writing.

The following examples are from mixed-ability classes. This ten-year-old had been with her family, she told me, to the Loire valley in western France. Wanting to impress someone, an imagined new friend perhaps, with the delights with which she was already familiar had set her writing at speed. Caliban's influence is obvious:

I'll take you to where green grapes grow in vineyards.
I'll show you sandmartins flying out of nests.
I'll take you to the ruins of a fairy castle.
I'll pick you ripe figs growing wild by the railway line.
I'll pour you Merlot, Chardonnay and Rosé
I'll show you wild herbs like mint and rosemary,
perfect for cold remedies.
I'll take you to a patisserie to smell the pain au chocolat cooking.
I'll play boules with you.
I'll cook you escargot and garlic for your tea.

Naomi

After all that French sophistication, the last three words are an English child coming down to earth.

A younger child wrote:

Forest
I'll fetch you fresh spring water.

You can touch crumbling leaves.
I'll hunt hare for you.
I'll show you badger holes.
You can climb the highest trees.
I'll show you scurrying moles.
You can watch birds swooping
through the swaying trees.
You can hear woodpeckers.
You can smell fresh bark.

Taye

Another child in a class of eight-years-olds remembered a holiday in southern Spain, and these are the evocative final lines of her writing:

I'll gather 32 fish on a pole so we can camp while they roast on
the pieces of burning coal I have found that day.

Jamie

One quiet girl in that class didn't volunteer any suggestions as the lesson started. Memories of Tunisia, Fuengirola, Tenerife, Florida, Disneyland Paris and Southwold (on the Suffolk coast near where these children live) were all flying about, but she was silent and let all that pass her by. Then she wrote (and this is her title):

My dreams

I will show you the berry volcano with sausages
I will get you a bouquet of flowers from the summery meadows
next to my house with lambs sunbathing
I will take you to the zoo to see the fluffy and cuddly koala bears
climbing up smooth trees
I will show you my divine berries hanging off the blossom trees
I will show you my dogs lying in the scorching sun that love me
every day and love to play

I will let you ride my horse with me when it is galloping along the
dull bark
I will let you hold the last ever egg of a blue eagle and wear my
feather mask
We will go to my park and play with my monkeys on the monkey
bars
I will show you my dragon and he will ride us to cloudland
I will show you the way out but remember me and don't doubt
what you think about

Leah

I prefer to print this piece as it was written: the lack of punctuation conveys something of the urgency of the writing, and we shouldn't trip a child up on technical matters when she is on a roll. And it must have taken some nerve on Leah's part, when everyone else was talking about exotic places, to have stuck with what's inside her head.

Leah's teacher told me that she wasn't usually a fluent writer: work from children identified in this way is always more of an achievement to me than anyone else's. Shakespeare is indeed for everybody, not just the conventionally clever.

Lesson Thirty-Five: Be not afear'd

And here is more from Caliban the poet. Later, in 3.2.130, Trinculo and Stephano are recovering from their binge on the liquor they have purloined from the ship. Suddenly, at ll.120–126, they are terrified ('O forgive me my sins!' 'Mercy upon us!') by Ariel's music 'on a tabor and pipe'. Caliban reassures them in his most famous lines:

> Be not afear'd, the isle is full of noises,
> Sounds, and sweet airs, that give delight and hurt not.
> Sometimes a thousand twangling instruments
> Will hum about mine ears; and sometime voices,
> That if I then had waked after long sleep,
> Will make me sleep again; and then in dreaming,
> The clouds methought would open, and show riches
> Ready to drop upon me, that when I waked
> I cried to sleep again.
>
> 3.2.130–138

I have found that this passage requires more preparation than usual, because the syntax is complicated. The lines from 'sometime voices' to the end present the most difficulty: I read them, emphasising the critical words – 'dreaming', 'clouds', 'open', 'riches', 'ready', 'drop', 'cried' – without worrying too much about the syntax. But if a paraphrase helps, it goes something like this:

There were voices so lovely that if I had dreamed them, I'd want to sleep again; and then, while I dreamed, the clouds would open and show riches ready for me; so that when I woke, I cried to sleep again.

Practice reading the lines to yourself a few times. Make sure, first, that you have got a grip on their meaning. Then read them aloud, concentrating on the alliterating sounds they make – for example, those *m*s and *n*s in the lines around the 'hum' of the instruments that Caliban can hear. Point out the repetition, and the assonance on the *ee* sound: 'sleep . . . me . . . sleep . . . dreaming . . . open . . . sleep again'. In great poetry, the music of the lines is as important as – and contributes to – their meaning; or, more exactly, the music and the meaning are intertwined.

Note the punctuation, especially after 'long sleep', and halt at each mark: perhaps you might pause there, as Caliban hesitates . . . looks around . . . wonders . . . remembers.

When you have read the lines a few times, read them to the class. Then ask the children to note that there are ten syllables, or occasionally nine or eleven, in each line. It is a remarkable fact that just pointing out the syllabic construction of the iambic pentameter, without necessarily talking about stress and foot (see Note I for more about this), and then reading some fine pentameters like these can edge children into making their own examples of this basic line of English poetry. Some of the children quoted below have written such lines.

Ask them: can they begin a poem with the words that Shakespeare has given them, 'Be not afear'd', or a modern version of them, and create a mysterious island in lines of nine, ten, or eleven syllables each?

The following three examples are by the apprentices:

Be not afeared, the light will guide you onwards.
Let the scene control your eyes, your looking.
Your eyes might as well be closed, just feel it.
You dream, you're there, in the frame, on the wall.
The lens grows, gets the full picture, only to
Shrink once back more, back into its shell, its home.
Once you've started, you can't stop; it's like you're stuck,
Stuck in my spell, you fill me with your memories.
Be not afeared, the light will guide you onwards.

Ruby

I had assumed that Shakespeare had invented the word 'twangling', but the *OED* assured me that he hadn't. He did invent many words, of course, and as they were writing while under the influence of this passage I invited the children to follow his example. Hence 'leafery' in Katie's poem which, though new, is not obscure, and 'scapes' in Ellie's: this writer has cleverly found a way of denoting views of both the land and the sea.

Anyway, I emphasised 'twangling', and similar sounds reverberated through some of the writing, as in this next piece ('entwine', 'sprung', 'tendrils', 'anguish'):

Be not afeared
for the vines of deception can entwine the mind here,
softly sprung wisps of gossamer whisper a thousand untruths
scents of befuddlement and mint,
leafery laced with bells and lace.
Strings of cobweb and pearls hang overhead,
tendrils scented with lilac mist scented with jasmine
and anguish gently shrouding the bejewelled glory.
Slow musical voices murmur.
Flee away from my woodland grove, I live here
in harmony and peace.
But you, you, oh yes, be afeared.

Katie

Be not afeared, just listen, listen.
White horses, blue meadows, soapy sands
advance and retreat, advance and retreat.
The lap and the child, tugging trouser legs
I hear lap, lap, tug, tug, lap, lap, tug, tug,
Dancing by moonlight and by day.
Picture scene beautiful, beautiful,
This is the isle of beauty scapes,
be not afeared, just listen, listen.

Ellie

This next example is from a ten-year-old in a mainstream class. I had suggested that they use other senses, not just hearing:

Be not afeared the island is full of spices.
The chilli floats in the air with others.
I hear people the crunching of people stepping on left-over black pepper on the floor.
The dragons are made of chilli and they are red hot.
There's no milk around here so you will have to cope with spice in your mouth forever.

Paolo

Lesson Thirty-Six: Pray you tread softly

This is such a simple lesson to teach. At 4.1.194, Caliban (though he doesn't know it) is leading Trinculo and Stephano to where they will be trapped by Prospero. He says: 'Pray you tread softly, that the blind mole may not hear a foot fall'.

Just that: so often in Shakespeare a single line will set children off.

> In this lesson, repeat the line a few times. Suggest that, if they want to, they might commit it to memory. Point out that most of the consonantal sounds are soft (pr, y, s, f, m, m, l, h). Then ask them to think of situations where to be very quiet is important. I collect ideas from them, such as wanting a baby to stay asleep. But in fact the children produced lines that were more resonant than that.

Leah, who appeared above inviting us into her dreams, and who was emerging as a writer already furnished with her obsessions, told me that she 'loved owls', and then wrote these lines. Shakespeare's words for Caliban had reached into her consciousness and enabled her to express something important about herself. Once again, she doesn't punctuate:

> *Please tread softly*
> *so that time won't have a clue to move*
> *so that wildlife and nature don't disappear*
> *so you don't scare the owls*
> *and the feathers won't fall off the owls*
> *so that the silence on the island stays silent*
> *so that a raindrop moves down a window*

Lesson Thirty-Seven: Knock a nail into his head

There's another side to Caliban, though, that isn't welcoming and full of poetry, and it's the most familiar one. Look at 1.2, and there's a ghastly creature, seen through Prospero's eyes: a 'freckled whelp, hag-born – not honoured with / A human shape . . .' Then, when we read 3.2, we see Caliban through his own words. He says to Stephano 'Bite him [Trinculo] to death, I prithee' (l.31). Later he tries to incite Stephano to murder Prospero while he is unconscious –

> I'll yield him thee asleep,
> Where thou mayst knock a nail into his head . . .
>
> ll.56–57

> I do beseech thy greatness, give him blows
> . . . beat him enough; after a little time
> I'll beat him too.
>
> ll.60, 78–79

And then:

> . . . with a log
> Batter his skull, or paunch him with a stake,
> Or cut his wezand with thy knife
>
> ll.84–85

This is the Caliban that the critic Harold Bloom says is the genuine one. That critic expresses exasperation at more sympathetic interpretations, and perhaps modern interpretations have gone too far that way, seeing him as what Bloom calls with heavy sarcasm 'our current noble rebel'. Anyway, if our children are to gain a foothold on understanding this character, they must encounter both the poet in the previous three lessons and the thug here.

Make sure that the children know some of the story from Caliban's point of view. The island belongs to him, bequeathed to him by his mother Sycorax. Much as Prospero believes that Antonio has stolen Milan from him, Caliban blames Prospero for the same crime, usurpation. Then act these lines, from 'I'll yield him thee asleep' to 'cut his wezand with thy knife' (that obscure word is 'windpipe'. And 'paunch' is 'stab in the belly'). Do this with blood-curdling mimes, if you can.

Ask the children, what sort of person is the Caliban who comes across in these lines? I think that, as often, discussing this in groups is a productive idea, before each group shares its findings with the whole class. Children talking among themselves about a topic that has been clearly presented to them, and without the constant supervision of adults, can be productive, because in such a setting they have opportunities and time to test theories with each other. Obviously, this model for learning will work better and better as they become accustomed to it. But you always have, of course, the whole-class option.

The children will readily pick up on Caliban's violence. But further questions about these lines should help them to see that he is a coward: he wants Prospero to be defenceless, and he wants his new 'friends' to strike first: 'yield him thee asleep/after a little time/I'll beat him too'.

I collected phrases written with Caliban's lines in mind. The apprentices wrote these with relish:

I'll distract him while you batter him with a wooden club. I'll tie him to a tree while you whip his face. You blind him while spraying pepper at him. While I hold his chair, you grab his legs and whip them so he falls over. Rip out his tongue and slap him with it. I'll hold him while you beat the life out of him. Cut off his ears with a butter knife. Take him up three miles on a rope then cut it.

Anon.

And Ayesha wrote:

> *I shall feed him wondrous drinks,*
> *yield him to sleep, then thou shall*
> *break his ribs, burn his clothes, and*
> *lay him to his death.*
> *I'll lay him down while you stretch him till he snaps.*

When I talked to her about this, she stated solemnly, belying all her behaviour to me and her colleagues in the group in the year or so that I have known her: 'I am a very violent person'.

Lesson Thirty-Eight: Blister you all o'er I

Prospero and Caliban hiss and shout and snarl insults at each other early on in the play. The work in this section will pay dividends later in terms of children's understanding of the two characters. Here are some extracts from 1.2.313–374, with Prospero's words in Roman type and Caliban's in Italic. Miranda is also on stage at this point – hence Caliban's 'Drop on ye both!':

. . . what ho! Slave! Caliban!
Thou earth, thou! Speak!

There's wood enough within.

Come thou tortoise . . . Thou poisonous slave . . .

As wicked dew as e'er my mother brushed
With raven's feather from unwholesome fen
Drop on ye both! A south-west blow on ye,
And blister you all o'er!

For this, be sure, tonight thou shalt have cramps,
Side-stitches that shall pen thy breath up, urchins
Shall, for that vast of night that they may work,
All exercise on thee; thou shall be pinched
As thick as honeycomb, each pinch more stinging
Than bees that made 'em.

. . .

All the charms
Of Sycorax – toads, beetles, bats – light on you . . .

110

Thou most lying slave

. . .

Filth as thou art . . .

I know how to curse. The red plague rid you
For learning me your language

Hag-seed, hence!
. . . malice . . .

I'll rack thee with old cramps,
Fill all thy bones with aches, make thee roar,
That beasts shall tremble at thy din . . .
So, slave, hence.

Ask the children to arrange themselves in pairs and to work on a radio production of these lines. They should first spend some ten minutes picking out keywords: 'tortoise', 'poisonous', 'unwholesome', 'blister' and the like, checking in dictionaries any obscure ones. As with the opening scene on board the ship, the words, rough and cruel in their impact as they are, do not need to be shouted. Draw from the children with questions other ways of speaking them: growling, hissing, snarling. Then ask each pair to perform their version to another pair.

Then they might make versions with movement. When each child plays Caliban, how does she or he suggest the suitability of Prospero's animal insults?

Once the children have become familiar with these insults, ask them to write their own. I've noticed over the years that there's much profit in asking children to do 'naughty' things in their writing. Sometimes I get them to write sentences that begin 'I don't like to boast, but . . .' which nevertheless end with an enormous boast ('I can skate round the rings of Saturn'); or I ask them to write sentences or poems that are made up of lies about the sun or the moon or water or a mirror ('The sun is an ice cube that will cool my drink'). Here, they are to write insults or curses that they wouldn't dream of speaking (not in adult company anyway), and it is liberating.

 Read Caliban's and Prospero's lines as viciously as you can (or as viciously as you dare).

I read them to a group of ten-year-olds, identified as 'ale writers', drawn from six schools. They wrote their curses:

May the sound of a baritone drift through your ears at night
and the tongue of a chameleon flick in your ears every second of your life
and the touch of electricity go through your body blue
and all the light disappear from your heart
and may your bright eyes turn grey and shrink to the size of a particle.

Daisy-Rose

Flooding in the West Country of the UK covered screens and newspapers around this time:

May every thunder cloud come upon you and every flood wash you
out.
May your house be brought down by every tornado
And as you go to sleep may all weathers come upon you.
When you walk in the sea the waters will drown you
and the strike of every lightning will be upon you
and the sun blind your every move.

William

Let the sound of the guitar flow through your earholes and into
your brain and let it churn it up like a squidgy boiled carrot.
Then let it flow out your nostrils like a runny pureray [purée]
filling the sizzling slimy saucepan. May the sharp sound of a
dead chord blister your heart and stop the constant flow of your
blood.

Sam

The next few pieces were written by children in a mainstream primary class, aged
8–9. They are, I suppose, less subtle, but just as strong. Indeed, their crude vigour
is an asset when writing in the character of Caliban, or at least the dark side of
that character:

You half pig, half toad
Piece of slop.
You one-eyed freak,
You unlovable creation.
 You live in the sewers you weed.
Who would love you?
I wish you were on the other side of the earth.
You should be extinct by now.

Lucy

You scowling snail
you slimy lizard
you are a disastrous dragon
you are a tremulous troll
you poisonous parasite
you stupid skunk
you will rot till there's nothing left of you
this curse will make your heart skip a beat.
                                             Bailey

Bouncy beanbag
a lot larger than a magic wand.
Animal-eating monster.
Killing machine.
I will put a curse on you with black stars to make you smellier
than you are now.
Horrible howling hawk.
Medieval monkey, evil over the land,
pimpled frog
sewer water drinker.
I can turn you into a volcano and when you erupt your lungs will
turn into ash and your heart into snails.
I wish you were Pinocchio with a duck (?duct)-taped mouth
I will turn you into a rubber book
It will be easier to get rid of you then.
                                             Faith

A Lithuanian child who had lived in England for two years, and who spent some of their time in the classroom acting as an interpreter between adults (including me) and more recent arrivals from Lithuania, wrote this:

CALIBAN TO PROSPERO
  you are gonna be squashed like a bug
rain of acid will burn you alive
a monster will eat
your blood will burst out of your body
snakes will poison you
your family will be in trouble
all of your books
will vanish and die
and last of all
you will die

                                    Ineeta

All nationalities of children will be inspired by Shakespeare's words if we present those words vividly.

Lesson Forty: An art lesson about Caliban

I've given broad instructions for art lessons based on the plays in the section on The *Dream*, so I'll just summarise here.

> The children should read all Caliban's lines in the first three acts of the play. There aren't very many. They should do this first individually, and then in groups. They should discuss what they have found out about him as they read, and mix their new information with what they discovered before – not least from their own writing.
>
> Ask them to pretend that they are in charge of the wardrobe department for a modern-day production of *The Tempest*. How will they dress Caliban? What parts of his character will they emphasise in their designs?
>
> Ask questions:
>
> - Will they stress the gentle side of Caliban that makes him say 'Be not afeared, the isle is full of noises', 'I'll show thee where the best springs are' and 'I'll dig thee pignuts'?
>
> - Or the violent side that makes him curse Prospero, and incite Stephano and Trinculo to kill him? They should also bear in mind Prospero's insults: 'tortoise . . . poisonous slave . . . thou earth . . . filth . . . malice . . .'
>
> They are also in charge of make-up, so when they draw their costumes for Caliban, they should draw his face fully made up – that is, in a typical expression.
>
> They might draw him in one of the following poses:
>
> - As he carries logs for Prospero (1.2.314)
>
> - As he curses Prospero (1.2.322–325)
>
> - As he drinks with Trinculo and Stephano (2.2.)

Figure 7.1 Caliban, by Raminta

- As he shows them where the 'best springs' are (2.2.146–150)

- As he says 'Bite him to death, I prithee' (3.2.32)

- As he tells Trinculo and Stephano about the island's strange noises (3.2.130)

They should write a brief note on their drawings telling us what part of the play they represent, and a relevant quote from the play.

8 'Merrily, merrily shall I live now'
Ariel

Is Ariel male or female? He is a spirit, 'a minister of fate', as he calls himself (3.3.60). Or perhaps he's an angel. He appears in the play in different shapes – a flaming light in the storm (Lesson Forty-One), a sea-nymph, a harpy at the banquet: so neither male nor female, really. I am going to use 'he' only for convenience, and because he is usually played by a male actor in modern productions (though that has not always been so). But the children should be aware throughout of his non-human quality. At 5.1.19, he himself makes it clear, not what he is, but what he is not. He tells Prospero that his affections for the king and his followers would become tender 'were I human'.

Ariel seems to be related to Puck in The *Dream* (see Chapter 2): he is another servant, or slave, with magical powers of movement who moves at speed at a master's will; who can subject mortals – the lovers and the mechanicals in The *Dream,* the survivors of the shipwreck in *The Tempest* – to his control. But Ariel has no mischief: indeed, any he might have had, and, indeed any humour, was squeezed out in a terrible pine tree. More of that later. He speaks his first important words to Prospero at 1.2.195–206.

Lesson Forty-One: The fire and cracks of sulphurous running

I boarded the king's ship. Now on the beak,
Now in the waist, the deck, in every cabin,
I found amazement. Sometimes I'd divide
And burn in many places; on the topmast,
The yards and bowsprit, would I flame distinctly,
Then meet and join. Jove's lightning, the precursors
O'th'dreadful thunderclaps, more momentary
And sight-outrunning were not; the fire and cracks
Of sulphurous running roaring the most mighty Neptune
Seem to besiege, and make the bold waves tremble . . .

When you teach this passage, the first task is to untangle the complex syntax of ll.6–8, from 'Jove's' to 'were not'. It isn't really difficult; with the last lines of the passage beginning 'Be not afeared', it was a matter of the order of the clauses, and it's the same here. Here is a paraphrase: 'I was quicker, more difficult to see, than Jove's lightning that comes before the thunder'. 'Beak' is a metaphor for the ship's prow. You may need to explain 'sulphurous' ('burning with a blue glow' is sufficient), but the way you say 'running roaring' will give away much of the spirit of the lines.

Once you have said these lines, explain that Shakespeare almost certainly had read an account of events on a ship published in 1610–1611. Here is part of that account:

An apparition of a little round light, like a faint star, trembling and streaming along with a sparkling blaze half the height upon the mainmast, and shooting sometime from shroud to shroud . . . and for three

or four hours together, or rather more, half the night it kept with us,
running sometimes along the mainyard and then returning.

This description of St Elmo's Fire is quoted in the Cambridge Schools Shakespeare edition of *The Tempest*. You might ask the children to research this
phenomenon on the Internet or in encyclopaedias. Usually appearing at the
tips of high objects – church spires, trees and, as here, masts, it's the glow
that accompanies discharges of electricity in the atmosphere. Often there is
a crackling noise as well.

   After discussing with the class what they have found out – first from their
research, second from studying Ariel's speech, and lastly from listening to the
contemporary account – brainstorm for words. The science, of course, was
unknown to Shakespeare's contemporaries. Ask the children what sailors in
the early seventeenth century might have made of the phenomenon; how they
may have reacted.

   Then ask the children to write their own poems about St Elmo's Fire.

These examples are by the apprentices. I am not sure why Ayesha set her writing
out like this:

> The fiery ball of electricity
>   ran alongside the hefty sailors' ship.
> The ghostly ball of lightning crackled
>   alongside the colossal sailors' ship.
> Quickly the blazing bundle of flames
> shot alongside the mammoth sailor's ship.
>
>   Ayesha

You dance
up on our masts,
fizz, crackle, bang goes your electricity,
flicker from
point to point

fizz, crackle, bang goes your electricity,
like spirits
arriving suddenly
fizz, crackle, bang goes your electricity,
creating ash,
sparks streaming, fizz, smoking,
bang goes your electricity,
you shoot us down!

                                      Ellie

Dancing	*flames*
Like twinkling	*stars above*
Smoking burnt	*wood high in the sky.*
Fumes like little	*lights at night.*
Above the fire	*invisible spirits.*
Golden glows fizz	*above the fire is*
Electric crackling	*sparking steaming.*
Shooting orange	*flames everywhere.*
Ghosts floating	*phantoms floating.*
Making blurs	*making blurs.*
Fizz, pop, bang.	*Fizz, pop, bang.*
	Kimberley

Re-reading these pieces during the final stages of making this book, it occurred to me that there is method or, perhaps it's a better word, *insight* behind the ways these writers have set their pieces out. Indeed, 'method' is a rather heavy word, altogether too grounded, too sound. These children felt that they needed nothing rooted. Like full stops. Regularity wasn't right. So Ayesha's unconventional left-hand margins, Ellie's flickering short lines, Kimberley's gaps and present participles . . . all these matched the 'flam[ing] distinctly' and the 'apparitions of a little round light' in both Ariel's speech and in the contemporary eye-witness account.

Lesson Forty-Two: In the cloven pine

Later in the same scene Prospero reminds Ariel about the state he was in when Prospero found him. The children will be interested in Ariel's horrible imprisonment. It's described by Prospero at 1.2.277–280. The witch Sycorax, Caliban's mother (so Prospero tells Ariel):

> did confine thee,
> By help of her more potent ministers
> And in her most unmitigable rage
> Into a cloven pine, within which rift
> Imprisoned thou didst painfully remain
> A dozen years . . .

The lines provide a vivid contrast to Ariel's anticipation of freedom, which comes later in the last act of the play ('Where the bee sucks', see Lesson Forty-Four). Indeed, teaching these two passages alongside each other might be valuable, not only for the mood and subject matter, but also for the contrasting effects conveyed by the sounds of the words.

Sometimes, I ask the children to listen hard to these lines and then to speak them after me. Listen, I suggest, to all the short 'i' sounds in the words 'within which rift / Imprisoned': how tight-fisted they are, how clipped, how miserable – compare them also to the big roaring air sounds in 1.1. They are imprisoned, or imprisoning words.

 But the main challenge here is to ask the children to draw the pine tree, and to depict Ariel imprisoned in it. They could do this in one of several ways.

- For example, they might take a semi-abstract approach to the figure of Ariel, merely suggesting the face in the trunk of the tree.
- Or they might show a hollowed-out tree, with the figure chained inside it.

- Or you might show them images of the Green Man. This mythological creature was certainly familiar to Shakespeare. Images of him are prominent in many churches, notably in the Chapter House of Southwell Minster in Northamptonshire. An unsmiling human face peers out between and among dense branches. Sometimes branches sprout from his nose, his mouth, his ears. This figure would provide a suitable model for Ariel in the tree.

- Or, best of all, but with all of those examples in mind, they might think of a way of their own.

Lesson Forty-Three: Full fathom five

In Shakespeare, I have noted before, high-status characters tend to speak in verse, low-status characters in prose. Caliban, as we have seen, though a low-status character, speaks in verse most of the time. We should bear this in mind when we decide what sort of person he is: he is not the usual clown or rogue, he is not like the rustic Athenians gathering in 1.2 of The *Dream*, he is not like the servants spoiling for a fight in the first scene of *Romeo and Juliet*.

What about Ariel? He never speaks in prose. His words often come in songs, and that fact tells us something about him: 'Air' is a synonym for 'song'. Here is his loveliest example:

> Full fathom five thy father lies,
> Of his bones are coral made;
> Those are pearls that were his eyes;
> Nothing of him that doth fade,
> But doth suffer a sea-change
> Into something rich and strange.
> Sea-nymphs hourly ring his knell.
> Hark, now I hear them, 'ding dong bell'.
> 1.2.396–403

The prince Ferdinand is on the island, 'Weeping again the king my father's wrack'. He hears music (it 'crept by me upon the waters') and asks: 'Where should this music be? I'the'air, or th'earth?' The song he hears ensures that the 'drowned father' remains in the front of his mind. How bleak and sad the words are: 'Of his bones are coral made; / Those are pearls that were his eyes . . . '

Some of the children will be thinking of *their* fathers and *their* grandfathers, sometimes even their great-grandfathers. I think about my father, my son, my fatherhood and my grandfatherhood. Some teachers tell me that they like to keep their private lives detached from their work. This seems to me to be a sad and false disconnection: anyway, when I teach these lines, a precious part of my life floods in.

> I have found that I have to prepare 'Full fathom five' with even more than the usual care: it deserves everything we can give. I make my voice descend during the first line, to mirror the meaning.
>
> I note the alliteration: those *f*s climaxing on the critical word 'father' and the sea-sound *ss* later on; I note, too, the assonance (sound similarities between vowels) between 'pearls' and 'eyes'; I emphasise that terrible phrase for a son who has lost his father: 'Nothing of him'.
>
> I ask the children what the words 'those are pearls that were his eyes' mean: the clue is in the whiteness of the pearls, and, in contrast, the colours of the iris. A child many years ago took my breath away when she said, haltingly, 'The colour came out of his eyes and they went grey like pearls.'

In some of these examples children have found themselves dealing with tragic (I know this sounds a little strong, but see it from their point of view) realities. They have taken those realties by surprise: lost grandparents, for example. Children as writers are prepared to travel bravely to emotional places; to take journeys, the prospect of which, usually, unnerves adults.

These children are in the same mixed-ability class of eight-year-olds as the Lithuanian girl Ineeta in Lesson Thirty-Nine (Chapter 7). With Ariel's song in their minds, they wrote:

Full fathom five my grandad's glasses lie
rusting away lying on the ocean floor
fish staring at my only memory
                              Bailey

Full fathom five my grandad's golden wedding ring lies
lying rusting to nothing

when it was brand new the sparkling light shone against it on his
finger
now hermit crabs are pinching it and throwing it
in the deep blue sea.

Cayden

Full fathom five my great grandma's jewels lie there on the stone.
They shine and now they rust.
Fish surround them.
Sharks swim through them.

Anon.

Full fathom five my mum's wedding dress lies
getting ript and half gone. Where is the other half?

Lucy

Full fathom
five my hermit crab
lies his shell
will break his
hard skin will
turn to stone
now I won't ever
see my little
friend again.

Joseph

I have printed these pieces as they were written because in several cases their layout seems to be a direction on how to read the poem. The next example shows a child who is not fluent with words but who is digging deep, with Shakespeare's help, half-consciously, into her emotions. Clerical correctness pales in its significance beside what this girl is trying (and, in part, succeeding) to convey:

Full fathom five my hunting kitten lies
it was like a family   little toy and
it was my famele her sparlk eyes she kulde up to me
sofa and I will never forget about her.

Lily

The group of apprentices responded like this. All the poems begin with 'Full fathom five':

. . . the thing I once loved,
the part of my life
that I sadly lost,
down down it sank right to the bottom
out of my reach

Sam

. . . my grandpa lies.
Under the ocean he lies
still as a rock and small as a snail
stiff as a slate and as freezing as the Antarctic.
There he lies, his body decaying in the sand.
His bones are as black as coal and as cold as ice.

Anon.

. . . under the sea my spirit lies, the hope and the wishes all just
gone, the dreams and brains just gone to waste, buried beneath the
lovely yellow sand. My spirit has just washed away, the hope and
the sighs just disappeared, the dreams and the brains. . .

Anon.

Lesson Forty-Four: Where the bee sucks

When Ariel anticipates his freedom he sings in 5.1 some lines that tell us much about him. He can flit, fly, skip, hide, all with ease. He is, as Prospero will call him later, 'my dainty Ariel':

Where the bee sucks, there suck I;
In a cowslip's bell I lie;
There I couch when owls do fly,
After summer merrily.
Merrily, merrily, shall I live now,
Under the blossom that hangs on the bough.

5.1.88–94

> When you say these words to the children, take Hamlet's advice to the players in 3.2 of his tragedy seriously: 'Speak the speech . . . trippingly on the tongue': the words need to skip lightly as the word 'trippingly' does. Emphasise the repetition of 'merrily'. Close-up images of summer flowers, bees and other insects would enrich this lesson.
>
> Then ask the children to imagine what freedom would be like to someone who had been, first, locked in a tree by a witch, and then been used as a slave by a powerful magician. Suggest that they might pretend to be tiny versions of themselves or some other creature, who can find refuge in any parts of nature.

These children are from a Year Four class:

I will drink from a coconut shell,
I will ride on a twirly snail shell,

I will be one of the tears of a baby,
I will sleep under the green leaf.
                              Samantha

I will sly [?slide] over the red dark roses and I'll drink the juice
from the big sweet raspberries.
I'll lie on the blossom that takes your breath away
and I'll make a house out of a bed of straw.
                                          Kobe

Under the rose there I sleep
with a leaf just like a blanket.
There I skip
up and down,
up and down
over the grass.
I eat some honey
that the bees keep.
When there's snow I'll make a snow angel.
                              Nour

I'll ride on a dragon over
The deep trees
I'll swim in the
Antarctic seas.
                    Zac

> Later, after giving the lesson a little more thought, I offered the apprentices a title and discussed the two adjectives in it at some length. I told them that they were going to write poems in praise of agility.

A dainty gymnastic poem for Ariel

I will live in the wing of the bumble bee.
Fly about on a big butterfly's body.

I will rest under the blossom trees.
Gracefully, gracefully, dancing under nature.
Gracefully, gracefully, spinning under nature.
I will live in the pip of an apple.
I will sleep in the scale of a butterfly's wing.
Gracefully, gracefully, dancing under nature.
Gracefully, gracefully, spinning under nature.
Gracefully, gracefully, sleeping under nature.
Gracefully, gracefully, sleeping under nature.

Kimberley

Where the rose petal curls is my parasol.
Where the woodpecker pecks is my music hall.
Here is my home and here I shall live
Peacefully, peacefully peacefully
For ever more.

Katie

Life as Ariel is small, delicate, a little butterfly fluttering by,
creeping through narrow spaces, slipping through holes like water,
little petal girl, Ariel, like a fit flower ready to burst.
Tears stream down her face when she cries, weeping fairy dust
and like a collar on a shirt she bends, flexible bouncy gymnast
disappearing through doors quick as a flash
as thin as a wisp of hair, poor little Ariel.

Lottie

I shall sit in an apple's pip,
hide, stand and sit,
flow with the sea's steady tide,
sand, sit and hide,
play with single grains of sand,
sit, hide and stand.

Ellie

Lesson Forty-Five: What's Ariel like? I

You might point out that the name is significant, reminding us of the word 'aerial', meaning 'of the air', one of the four elements. You could talk about the others: earth, fire and water. You might point out the contrast with Caliban. Ask: what would his main element be? Give reasons for your choice. And what element, apart from air is Ariel? There's seems to be no earth in him; but fire? Water?

By now, the children will be familiar with much of Ariel's part in *The Tempest*. Revise the speech about the fire in the rigging (Lesson Forty-One), the songs 'Full fathom five' (Lesson Forty-Three) and 'Where the bee sucks' (Lesson Forty-Four); and ask them to brainstorm for adjectives that describe Ariel's personality. I like to do this in stages. First, the children close their eyes and think for a good minute or even more, searching for adjectives in their minds. Then, in groups of five or six, they should pool what they have found and then search for more. Finally, a plenary session rounds the lesson off.

Harold Bloom (1999) brings the words 'angel' and 'spirit' into his discussion of the play. Both these words suggest sexlessness. Ask the children to discuss: would their Ariel be played by a male or a female actor? Again, they must give reasons for their choice.

Lesson Forty-Six: What's Ariel like? II

This lesson gives children an opportunity to read carefully with a clear objective: if they examine everything that Ariel has said or sung in the play – or at least revised their work on him so far – they will be able to write their own poem. When they have read all, or most of his lines, they should write a poem with the following structure: 'I may not be Ariel, but I can . . .'

The second line of each verse should be something that would be characteristic of Ariel, but not something in the play. The children will probably focus on his movement, his speed, his willingness to obey Prospero; but they might also make up lines about his music, his power (they might recall the lines about St Elmo's Fire in Lesson Forty-One) and other aspects of him that occur as they read his part.

This child is eight years old:

> I may not be Ariel
> but I can see myself with no mirror in front of me
> and I can thread a needle with no struggle at all.
> I can make lava from the most famous volcano to come out of the
> palm of my hand.
>
> Jamie

Some other examples by several children:

> I may not be Ariel, but

I can make you a part of a jigsaw puzzle . . . I can shrink down so small that Santa puts me in my own stocking . . . I can bring my nan back to life and make her happy . . . I can fly to the moon and come back to the door of the Taj Mahal . . . I can ride on a bee like it's a roller coaster . . . I can be candle flame shaking . . . I can scare sailors with my nightmare light . . . I can shoot from the depths of the sea to the top of the highest mountain.

This structure will also work well for Puck in *A Midsummer Night's Dream.*

Lesson Forty-Seven: Ariel – An art lesson

See my earlier lesson on designing a costume for Puck (Chapter 2, Lesson Ten). Now, the children should revise everything they have discovered about Ariel by re-reading all his lines. (If this sounds to them like a daunting task, reassure them: there aren't many!) They might do this individually, and then by sharing what they have found in pairs or in groups.

As a product of their reading, they should pretend to be wardrobe designers, and draw costumes for Ariel. They must bear in mind that he is agile and moves very fast. How will they show this in the way they draw both the character and the clothes?

9 'Three Minor Characters'
Francisco, Gonzalo and Iris

Lesson Forty-Eight: Beating the surges

Shakespeare writes powerful lines for minor figures, like Francisco. In 2.1, the king has just been stranded on the island with his courtiers. We have already seen Ferdinand mourning his father as he listens to Ariel singing 'Full fathom five' ('of his bones are coral made'). Now that scene is mirrored with one in which the father mourns his son: 'O thou mine heir // What strange fish / Hath made his meal on thee?' One of his followers, Francisco, has only these lines to speak in the whole play. From l.108 onward he gives us one of the best descriptions of a swimmer:

Sir, he may live.
I saw him beat the surges under him,
And ride upon their backs; he trod the water
Whose enmity he flung aside, and breasted
The surge most swol'n that met him. His bold head
'Bove the contentious waves he kept, and oared
Himself with his good arms in lusty stroke
To th'shore, that o'er his wave-worn basis bowed,
As stooping to relieve him. I not doubt
He came alive to land.

2.1.108–117

> ↪   Note that words can be tired or weak: 'lay', for example, or 'sat' both lack energy in their sounds as well as their meanings. When you teach this speech, act it yourself, emphasising those muscular verbs: 'beat', 'ride', 'trod', 'flung', 'breasted' and 'oared'. They're mostly easy to visualise, and someone will understand 'oared' either with the help of your acting or without. Then ask the children to mime each of the actions before they write.

These children were members of a top literacy set:

The swimmer

He heaved his way across to the shore.
He thrashed with his palm.
The blue water blinded his eyes
but he did not give up at all.
He swayed his arms and legs weaving in and out.
There he struck against the water
breathing heavily in and out.

Halima

He flung his arms across the rough seas.
He smashed his legs against the waves.
He hacked at the water like an Olympic swimmer.
He barged into the tsunami.
He crashed his body through the wildest waters.

Farida

He soared through the water,
tearing it this way and that,
leaving a frenzy of ripples behind,
driving, peddling and splashing through, then at last he

finished his goal, a crowd of cheering people
praising his impossible task.

Mustafa

I pointed out to that writer that his piece was all one sentence and he said, 'I know': he had intuited that something of the effect of a swimmer's progress through water would have been lost had there been a full stop after, say, 'splashing through'. The same goes for all those –ing words.

He pushed and he pulled as he swam through the sea.
And he didn't look back, only forward.
And he heaved and he hoed like a pirate hoisting a sail
And he thrashed at the waves like a humming bird's wings.
He avoided the crash of the waves.
He skidded between the foam from the crashes.

Eloise

This writer chose the present tense. The effect of this is that the king (and we) see the prince live and powerful in the water as if it's happening now:

The swimmer he...
rows himself along the smashing waves
his arms push along the gusty waves
heaves in and out of the thrashing surges
his muscles all tightened, of getting washed away
is never frightened
ignores the strong waves pushing up against him
doesn't care, just wants to accomplish it
blocks the waves with his tense strong muscles
weaves through the water even when it is strong

Rohan

Your boy,
he threw his arms out
jumping the waves like a dolphin,
not a breath left within him
but pushing onwards.
With one last jump
he reached land,
I'm sure of it Sir,
I'm sure.

Jessie

Finally, a boy in another school wrote this. His handwriting was clenched. I think both his underlining and his spaces are there for good reasons, so I reproduce them both here:

In his eyes

We were panicking aboard the ship
crying for our loved ones.
When I saw him, I saw a man
his blond hair glimmering in the moonlight,
the waves smashing   against him
in his eyes I saw no fear. I saw courage.

Matthew

Lesson Forty-Nine: All things in common

Shakespeare has already introduced Gonzalo in the first scene of the play as a decent old man. During the storm, he is mocked by the plotters Sebastian and Antonio, but he is staunch in his good humour, his stoicism and his support for his king. As a preliminary to some study of this man, here are some of the words that he says in that first scene, when everyone's lives are in danger:

> The king and prince at prayers! Let's assist them,
> For our case is as theirs . . .

> Now would I give a thousand furlongs of sea for an acre of barren
> ground – long heath, brown furze, anything. The wills above be done,
> but I would fain die a dry death.

In 1.2., we find that when, years before the opening of the play, Prospero was cast adrift with the baby Miranda, Gonzalo had 'furnished' Prospero 'with volumes that / I prize above my kingdom'. At 5.1.68 Prospero calls him 'good Gonzalo'.

The man's naive decency emerges here at 2.1.143–151, where he describes his ideal state, his perfect country, his dream world, his utopia, his (in the words of an old American folk song) 'Big Rock Candy Mountain':

> . . . no kind of traffic
> Would I admit; no name of magistrate;
> Letters should not be known; riches, poverty,
> And use of service, none; contract, succession,
> Bourn, bound of land, tilth, vineyard, none;
> No use of metal, corn or wine, or oil;
> No occupation, all men idle, all;
> And women too, but innocent and pure;
> No sovereignty –
>
> . . .

All things in common nature should produce
Without sweat or endeavour. Treason, felony,
Sword, pike, knife, gun or need of any engine
Would I not have . . .

Here is a paraphrase:

I will have no transport; no law system; schools and universities will not be known; there will be neither rich people nor poor, and neither slavery nor servants; lands will not be inherited; boundaries, fences and agriculture will be unknown . . . everyone will have leisure, and everything will be owned in common, and nature will give her produce without working; there'll be no crimes, no weapons of any kind; nature will feed my innocent people freely.

> Ask the children to think hard about all these lines, and to come up with four adjectives to describe what they know of this character. They should, as usual, do this in the silence of their own thoughts at first, and then share them in groups and, finally, with the whole class.
>
> Ask them to make their own ideal states, their perfect countries, their dream worlds, their utopias.

I'll have no school, writing, teachers
I'll have no illness, coughs or colds
I'll have no snow, rain or clouds
I'll have cars, trucks, motorbikes
I'll have cows, monkeys, pigs, cats, dogs
I'll have all the people to be rich
I'll have no buses, trains, helicopters or boats
I'll have no rude words or rude people
I'll have no sea, rivers or lakes
I'll have friends, shops and drinks
I'll have everyone having a family
I'll have every colour in the world like red

I'll have orange, black, silver, white gold
I'll have no churches
I'll have no books, no magazines
                                        John

As so often in the writing I quote in this book, we get a glimpse of children's anxieties: 'I'll have everyone having a family' is an example here.

There shall be no robbing, stealing, kids crying, anger, and no more killing. No more piranhas, stingrays, eels, whales, sharks but there shall be innocent bugs, cute little pets, gorillas, chimpanzees, orang-utans and apes. There shall be whispering oceans, seas and salt water. There shall be no guns, knives, swords, axes or chainsaws, or any other weapons. There shall be six musical waterfalls just a mile away, all singing jazz, brass, opera around the corner, and rock and country. At the bottom of the waterfall is a slide that whispers into the waterfall's ear. There shall be seven artists in my house, Van Gogh, Monet, Picasso, Me, Alfie and Ben and Joseph.
                                        Anon.

One could further enrich this lesson by quoting from the book of Isaiah in the Old Testament. This is a passage with which Shakespeare would certainly have been familiar:

They shall beat their swords into plowshares, and their spears into pruning hooks; nation shall not lift up sword against nation, neither shall they learn war any more . . .

The wolf shall also dwell with the lamb, and the leopard shall lie down with the kid; and the calf and the young lion and the fatling together; and a little child shall lead them . . .

They shall not hurt or destroy in all my holy mountain . . .

Isaiah Chapter 2 verse 4; Chapter 11 verses 6–7, 9 (King James Bible)

These eight-year-olds had heard those lines, as well as some lines from an American folk song that have been in the back of my mind almost all my life. Here is a snatch of it, enough to give the flavour:

> O the buzzing of the bees and the chocolate trees
> The soda water fountain
> Where the lemonade springs and the blue bird sings
> In the big rock candy mountain . . .

I put that in the mix with the Gonzalo and the Isaiah. Here are some excerpts from writing by a mixed-ability class of eight-year-olds:

> In my perfect world there will be sunshine every day and every girl will rule the world and all the boys will be servants . . . The sweet cows play in the short green grass and the pigs entertain you as the beautiful sun sets and the horses will run around you, you will hear them making noises but it won't be very loud, there won't be anything coming down from the sky . . . I will have a palace but nobody will be poor, everyone will get to live in a palace and have servants and there will only be one job and that will be training to be a servant or actually being a servant . . . dumbness is allowed . . . smoking is against the law . . . maths will not exist and will just be a myth . . . no-one will dye their hair or have tattoos . . . no-one will be called dumb or smart as such words will be illegal and no-one will blow their own trumpets or send flowers to themselves and time shall not be a problem as there will be no day or night . . . Stealing will never happen for to the city of thieves they shall go . . . there will be a swimming pool made out of chocolate and slush puppies . . . maybe some jelly lakes or flower drinks . . .

In these sentences, there are echoes of all the passages. First, there's Gonzalo's naive idealism: '. . . nobody will be poor, everyone will get to live in a palace and have servants and there will only be one job and that will be training to be a servant or actually being a servant . . .' Second, the childlike hedonism of the American folk song appears in: 'sunshine every day . . . a swimming pool made out of chocolate and slush puppies . . . maybe some jelly lakes or flower drinks . . .' And finally, compare the haunting line 'there won't be anything coming down from the sky' (more evidence of a child writing about a worry) with Isaiah's 'They shall not hurt or destroy in all my holy mountain'.

Lesson Fifty: Queen of the sky

A masque was, in Shakespeare's time, a court entertainment involving great expense – Gibson (1995) tells us that James I spent £20,000 on one, equivalent to over a million pounds today. There would have been poetry, music, dance and complicated stage machinery and lighting. I suppose if one thinks of the closing ceremony of the London Olympics in 2013, one gets the general idea, though masques would have only been for the inner circle of society.

Prospero has arranged this masque for his daughter Miranda and her lover Ferdinand ('A contract of true love to celebrate' l.84). Iris, the goddess of rainbows, appears. That rainbow stands for the end of the storm, of course, but even more, it stands for reconciliation between Prospero and Alonso, and between characters in general: this coming together is a characteristic of all Shakespeare's late romances. Even Prospero and Caliban speak kindly to each other at 5.1.291–294:

PROSPERO　　　　　　　　　As you look
To have my pardon, trim it handsomely.

CALIBAN Ay, that I will; and I'll be wise hereafter,
And seek for grace.

When I was thinking about children writing under the spell of this play, some lines of Iris and Ceres jumped out: they are epithets (a Greek word meaning 'something added . . . an adjective or adjectival phrase defining an attribute' according to Gray (1984)). Here's what Iris calls the rainbow: 'queen o'th'sky' . . . 'watery arch'. There are more epithets: Ceres calls Iris 'many-coloured messenger' with 'saffron wings', 'rich scarf to my proud earth' and mentions 'thy blue bow', 'heavenly bow' (4.1.1–84).

This is such a straightforward lesson to teach. Once you have introduced the children to those epithets ask them to close their eyes, cover them up and think. Hold them to this silent thought for as long as feels right – and, from my experience, the longer the better. Ask them to think of phrases that might be suitable for describing a rainbow.

These emerged in a brainstorming session, and I scribbled them down as the class called them out:

Unicorns' valley of heaven... Colourful skipping rope... Letter C... Multi-coloured magic cloud... Bouncy slide belt... Bridge to the mystical world of Asgard... Five angels swinging down... Queen of colour and world...

For more on epithets, see Lesson Fifty-Six in Chapter 10 on *Romeo and Juliet*. Finally, some words about Prospero and Miranda.

Lesson Fifty-One: My magic garment

Prospero is not, of course, a minor character; but he is not a character accessible to children either. This activity can make him clearer.

> Offer them the following lines and suggest that they design costumes for him. They should write captions on their drawings about the aspect of his character their drawings show – quotations from his lines, perhaps. Here are some that will help:

At 1.2.23 Prospero is just back, we presume, from stage-managing the storm, and he says to Miranda, like any man just home from an arduous task who is accustomed to obedience from his child:

Lend thy hand
And pluck my magic garment from me . . .

Ask the children to draw Prospero as he braces his body – shoulders lifted, arms hanging straight down – for Miranda to take his 'magic garment' from him.

Or ask them to draw him as he controls the storm, wearing or carrying everything he needs for his magic.

Or as he (1.2.137) confronts Caliban: 'Come, thou tortoise'

Or, alone with his daughter, as he tells Miranda the story of how they came to the island: 'Canst thou remember / A time before we came unto this cell?' 1.2).

Figure 9.1 Prospero, by Madeline

Lesson Fifty-Two: O brave new world!

As the play ends, Miranda sees all the men (except Trinculo and Stephano) who have been saved from the sea, as well as Ferdinand, with whom she has fallen in love. At 5.1.182–184, in her innocence she exclaims:

> O wonder!
> How many goodly creatures are there here!
> How beauteous mankind is! O brave new world
> That hath such people in it!

The lines, of course, are full of dramatic irony. You might point out that among these 'goodly creatures' in this 'brave new world' there are usurpers and would-be murderers.

These lines offer a final opportunity for writing. First, ask the children to read this speech carefully, noting down what they think are the most important words. Then in groups of five or six, they should take turns reading it aloud, emphasising, perhaps, those words. How can each child express 'wonder'? They might think about what they might do at each punctuation mark, especially at the three exclamation marks. How long might they pause for? At 'beauteous mankind', they might look around at each other as if they were, indeed, beauteous.

Then ask them to write a poem with the same words to begin it, 'O wonder!' or 'O brave new world'. This must be a poem that celebrates any human aspect of the world we live in. Photographs of people from all over the world – the kind of photograph that the *National Geographic* magazine has been printing for decades – make a wonderful follow-up for Miranda's lines.

I showed some children *In Focus: National Geographic's Greatest Photographs* (see References), and one of the apprentices, as much influenced by the photographs as by Miranda's speech, wrote:

Oh brave new world
that gives us children and lets them grow strong into:
explorers, musicians, cooks and doctors.
Oh brave new world!

Oh brave, new, world
that brings us hope
that lets us believe, aspire and gives us faith.
Oh brave new world!

Oh brave, new, world
that gives us identities so we know who we are
who makes us different to each other.
Oh brave new world!

Ayesha

Star-crossed Lovers: Romeo and Juliet

A summary

There's no need to look further than the opening lines of the play for a summary of the plot. Here is a paraphrase of the Prologue:

There were two noble families in the city of Verona. They had borne each other a grudge for generations. This grudge came to life again at a time when a member of one of them, Romeo, a Montague, fell in love with a member of the other, Juliet, a Capulet. This made Juliet's father rage with anger. The story of the play tells how, in their deaths, they brought peace to the city.

All we might add is that Mercutio, who was a member of neither family, also had a fate bound up in the quarrel; and that a Friar's good intentions contributed to the story's tragic end.

***

This part of my book focuses on *Romeo and Juliet*. First there is the wordplay that permeates all of it (Chapter 10): without some understanding of this, no understanding of this play is possible. Then there is the character of Mercutio and his Queen Mab (Chapter 12); and finally the central characters (Chapter 13) plus the father of one of them, Lord Capulet. Chapter 11 has lessons on how the Prologue is a spoiler, on some invitations to a party, and the first violence in the play.

There is a practical reason for choosing this play. Many of our children will be studying it at secondary school, and it seems to be useful to familiarise them at an earlier age with some of the play's characters and their poetry. And it is the one Shakespeare play about which everyone seems to know something: its love story is one of the central myths that inform the way we think about young people and the nature of love between men and women.

But the play isn't only about love. Another and equally dominant theme in *Romeo and Juliet* is death. From curtain up to the end of 1.2, 'death', and related words – 'fatal', 'bury', 'end', 'grave', 'dead', 'die', as well as words to do with violence – 'blood', 'bloody' 'purple fountains' appear some fifteen times. And of course this intensifies as the play progresses. Even the jokes – Mercutio's cracks at Romeo's expense at 2.4.12 ('poor Romeo, he is already dead, stabbed with a white wench's black eye) are death-marked, and his pun on 'grave' as he lies dying is always shocking.

One insurmountable problem with the play, as far as teachers and children in primary schools are concerned, is it's bawdy. I have written about this in Note G.

10 Star-crossed, brawling loves, fiery Tybalt . . . and a grave man

There's one feature of *Romeo and Juliet* that's worth teaching early in children's schooling. They should get a grip on the frequent use of, and the richness of, its wordplay. The value of learning about compound adjectives, oxymorons, epithets and puns arises from the fact that, first, children find the first three easy to grasp; and second, they open a window on much of the nature of the language of the play. In fact working with tricks of language at ages eight to eleven sheds a light on the language generally of Shakespeare's early work that will stand our children in good stead for later on – in some cases for the rest of their lives.

There are four broad categories of wordplay here: compound adjectives ('Star-crossed'), oxymorons ('brawling lovers'), epithets ('fiery Tybalt') and puns ('grave man').

Lesson Fifty-Three: Star-crossed – Compound adjectives

Romeo and Juliet gets much of its flavour from the frequency and richness of its compound adjectives and a subset of that group, the negated adjective. Some are partly hidden from us by their familiarity, especially the negated adjectives: 'untimely', 'unworthy', 'dishonourable', 'unaccustomed' among others; though it's worth bearing in mind that, although they may be parts of everyday speech to us – compound adjectives rinsed of their original power – they will have been more forceful in Shakespeare's time: 'dishonourable' for one example, will have carried immense force – consider the word in the context of 'family honour', both for Shakespeare's contemporaries and for many of our own.

Most, though, are still fresh, striking in conveying much of the mood of this play. Here is a select list, scene by scene:

The Prologue: unclean, star-crossed, misadventured, death-marked.

1.1: neighbour-stained (the Prince's powerful description of the blades of used swords), all-cheering, well-seeming, still-walking, saint-seducing (the last three Romeo's words)

1.2: Earth-treading, well-apparelled (it emerges that Capulet is fond of compound adjectives), all-seeing (as is Romeo)

1.3: dove-house, high-lone (one Shakespeare invention that hasn't survived except here, meaning 'all alone'), unbound

1.4: without-book, grey-coated, dew-dropping, untimely (the last is Romeo's again, the others Mercutio's)

1.5: unwashed, unplagued, unlooked-for, well-governed, ill-beseeming (the last four are Capulet's)

Chorus: new-beloved

2.2: unadvised (Juliet), flattering-sweet, silver-sweet (these two are Romeo's), loving–jealous (Juliet)

2.3: grey-eyed, precious-juiced, unstuffed, distemperature, misapplied (all Friar Lawrence)

2.4: single-soled (Romeo), wild-goose (Mercutio)

2.5: nimble-pinioned, wind-swift (Juliet)

3.1: dishonourable, fire-eyed (Romeo)

3.2: fiery-footed, love-performing, sober-suited, black-browed, death-darting, dove-feathered, wolvish-ravening, maiden-widowed (all of these are Juliet's)

3.3: unworthy, sharp-ground, heart-sick , mist-like (all Romeo), ill-beseeming, dis-membered, mis[be]haved (all the Friar's)

3.5: discord, ill-divining, dispraise, unaccustomed (Juliet, though used by Lady Capulet, too, some thirty lines later), tempest-tossed, green-sickness, (both Capulet)

4.1: long-experienced, new-made, unstained (all Juliet)

4.2: unfurnished, self-willed (Capulet)

5.1: soon-speeding, life-weary (Romeo)

5.3: unhallowed, savage-wild (Romeo), unsubstantial, inauspicious, world-wearied, unsavoury, mis-sheathed (Capulet)

Before you show the children this list, arrange them in five groups, and allot each group an act. Each group should scour its act, looking for and writing down all the compound adjectives. Do the Prologue spoken by the Chorus yourself as an example. One suggestion for the children: simply watch out for hyphenated words, and the negative prefixes 'un-' and 'dis-'.

Lesson Fifty-Four: Neighbour-stained

 Ask the children to write tiny poems with compound adjectives in them. They must not, of course, plagiarise any of Shakespeare's.

The apprentices wrote these. They were by now quite familiar with much of the play, having written in the grip of its poetry. Inevitably, there was going to be melodrama! But if you can't be excused a little going over the top when you are eleven, when can you be?

> *Their mis-made souls*
> *Made them cold-footed*
> > *Ellie*

> *Black-hearted and dull-spirited*
> *she walked away.*
> *Love-beaten she lay on the ground*
> *and took her last terror-stricken breath.*
> > *Savannah*

> *He walked to school heavy-footedly.*
> *The girl with a muddled soul was full of disappointment.*
> > *Lauryn*

Lauryn's first line is an unconscious echo of the Seven Ages of Man speech in *As You Like It*: 2.7: 'And then the whining school-boy, with his satchel, / And shining morning face, creeping like snail / Unwillingly to school'. This miserable, scrubbed boy is evidently part of a folk-memory even for those who, like Lauryn, don't know *As You Like It*.

The richly-painted peacock strolled through the tunnel-mouthed crowd.

Xavie

His mis-read soul made my heart tremble.
Heel-winged and life-weary was the messenger of God.
Black-brained and granite-hearted was the hatred-wired monster.
The smile-bearing girl's spirit was a caged butterfly.

Katie

My blood-smothered hands made me terrified to place the daggers on the guards.

Evie

That eight-year-old had, she told me, just read an abridged version of *Macbeth*. Lines in 5.2 had certainly made an impression.

His wise-eyed look made me sheath my battle-weary iron.
Her blaze-hearted mind made me love-scattered.
Her wise-eyed look made me love-scattered.

Evan

The silent-pursed lady's
still standing there hunger-filled
waiting in her mismatched slippers.
Her tear-soaked hankie is with him
there in 'the box' as she calls it
whenever her grief-stricken face dares.

Ruby

Ruby always takes on any challenge; and she never fails to bend it to her will. 'Silent-pursed', and the inverted commas around 'the box', go some way beyond what we expect from a ten-year-old.

The swiftly-agile blue tit made me forget all my worries.
The lightning-robber sprinted away from the bank in the darkness.

Evan

And, eccentrically:

My electrically-laced shoes
made me have cold worn-out hands
every time I ran a race.

Lee

Lesson Fifty-Five: Brawling love – Oxymorons

The second category of wordplay is the oxymoron. Shakespeare was familiar with poems written in the classical tradition that, as Gray says, 'express the pangs of love via contradictory states: "I burn and freeze like ice"'. Almost all of Romeo's early words are oxymorons and this fact should tell us something about his character. He's complaining to his friend Benvolio about the misery caused by his unrequited love for Rosaline:

> . . . O brawling love, O loving hate,
> O any thing of nothing first create!
> O heavy lightness, serious vanity,
> Misshapen chaos of well-seeming forms,
> Feather of lead, bright smoke, cold fire, sick health,
> Still-waking sleep, that is not what it is!
> This love I feel, that feel no love in this.
>
> 1.1.167– 173

Later, Juliet hears the terrible news that her new love, Romeo, is responsible for the death of her kinsman Tybalt. The fact that she too is free with this figure of speech suggests that she has much in common with Romeo:

> JULIET O serpent heart, hid with a flow'ring face!
> . . .
> Beautiful tyrant, fiend angelical!
> Dove-feathered raven, wolvish-ravening lamb!
> Despised substance of divinest show!
> Just opposite to what though justly seem'st,
> A damned saint, an honourable villain!
>
> . . .

O that deceit should dwell
In such a gorgeous palace!

3.2.73–85

To understand what an oxymoron is helps children to understand a significant part of the technique of early Shakespeare, and adds a dimension to their writing.

> Read the speeches given above, emphasising the contradictions in each phrase. You could, for example, merely breathe the word 'feather' and growl 'lead'; do much the same with 'heavy' and 'lightness'. You could mime sickness and health on 'sick health'. . . and so on. Children might be directed to an oxymoron in *The Tempest*. At 3.3.38, Alonso refers to 'an excellent dumb discourse'; and in *A Midummer Night's Dream* Hippolyta refers to 'So musical a discord' to describe the baying of hounds (4.1.115). You could quote the famous oxymorons from *Macbeth*: 'So foul and fair a day I have not seen' (1.3.39) is Macbeth's first line; 'Lesser than Macbeth, and greater' and 'Not so happy, yet much happier' follow from the weird sisters' mouths. Ask the children to write their oxymoronic poems.
>
> You could back this up with examples from other literature: one from Milton's description of Hell, for example, 'darkness visible', (*Paradise Lost* Book 1, l.63)

I collected these in my notebook from a class:

A hollow heart
That loves with hate.
Black fire that heats with coldness.
Manufactured nature
Which is red and shrinks
With an uncolourful rainbow.
Heavy air which determinedly tries to push down.
A solid bubble that floats down fast and then pops.
Hot rain falls from the sun and disappears in mid-air.
A solid ghost always forgets not to walk through walls.
An oxymoron is not an oxymoron.

The writers in the next group were in a set of children who were presented to me as children 'at the higher range of ability . . . pushing towards a higher level'. I had asked them, first to write oxymorons based on Romeo's and Juliet's, and then to develop them, either by adding another example, or by extending one with a connective:

> One-sided love at first sight makes me feel sad affection.
> One-sided love at first sight makes me feel joyful hatred.
> One-sided love at first sight makes me Cupid's loathing.
> One-sided love at first sight makes me like life is dying.

That writer had another go in the same session:

> My hateful love is like clocks going anti-clockwise.
> Unfriendly friendship to me is like a flattened ball.
> My friends who are not friends are like burning ice.
> Friends who hate me are like unplaying music.
> > Vidushi

> Flaming ice to me is like a melting sun.
> Flaming ice to me is burning water.
> > Suraiya

> The hatred of friends
> Makes me forgive their crime,
> Makes my ominous feeling joyful.
> This all makes me dead but alive.
> > Kuljeet

> Blindness to sight makes me feel
> Like God's forgiveness.

> Sight to blindness make me feel
> Like God's punishment.
> > Mayeesha

Suddenly, I am reminded of an extended oxymoron in St Matthew's Gospel, where Jesus tells his disciples 'He that findeth his life shall lose it: and he that loseth his life for my sake shall find it.' (Chapter 10, verse 39). I will read this to the next group of children with whom I do this lesson.

> Ask the children to study Juliet's last speech in 5.3 and to find what is a truly shocking oxymoron. The complete speech is: 'Yea, noise? Then I'll be brief. O happy dagger, / This is thy sheath; there rust, and let me die.' (lines 169–170): it's 'happy dagger', of course. Ask the children to invent similarly shocking examples.

Here are some examples from a class of eight- and nine-year-olds, noted down as they called them out. I printed them in the order in which they came. I think it makes a revealing and rather grim little poem:

happy swearword
best friend cancer
grinning cigarette
delightful bombs
joyful bow and arrow
glorious knife
wonderful gunfire
happy rifle
life-saving AK47
devil's fork
funny bazooka
fun-filled axe

Of course, the US Military have already given the world a prime example of an oxymoron. When a soldier is inadvertently killed by his own side, it is 'friendly fire'.

Lesson Fifty-Six: The fiery Tybalt: Epithets

The fiery tybalt.

More than the Prince of Cats.
One, and two, and a third in
your bozum!

Ellie Barker.

Figure 10.1 The fiery Tybalt, by Ellie Barker

The *Shorter Oxford English Dictionary* defines an epithet as an 'adjective express-ing some quality or attribute regarded as characteristic of a person or a thing'. Homer's examples are the most frequently quoted: 'rosy-fingered dawn', for exam-ple, and one that I have occasionally tried to imagine – and failed – while holding a glass of red in a Greek beach restaurant: 'the wine-dark sea' – sunrise or sunset off the coast of an Aegean island, perhaps?

In *Hamlet*, in order to show us that the play within the play is dated, Shake-speare puts Homeric epithets of the kind that was quickly going out of fashion at the time into the mouth of the Player King in 2.2:

The rugged Pyrrhus . . . the hellish Pyrrhus . . . reverend Priam . . . the mobled [Warwickshire for 'muffled'] queen.

> This is a straightforward lesson. Simply tell the children the examples above, and this further example from Homer's *Iliad* that was so effective that, even in translation, it has becomes a cliché: 'winged words'. Write them up perhaps, and then come to the example at 1.1.100, where Juliet's kinsman is described by Benvolio as 'the fiery Tybalt'. Suggest that the children find their own epithets for historical characters.

The children quoted here are from several schools, all labelled as gifted, and working together under one roof for a day:

The magical Shakespeare.
The adventurous Shakespeare.
The ambitious Boudicca.
The flaming Boudicca.
The cruel Henry VIII.
The unhearted Henry.

(That is an example of an epithet and a compound adjective in one.)

The inspirational Rosa Parks.
The life-changing Harriet Tubman.
The noble Gandhi.

Or, I suggested, they might choose epithets for their contemporaries. The Olympics were still a recent memory:

The lightning Bolt

I don't know if the pun was intentional.

The mind-blowing Jessica Ennis.

The pathetic Justin Bieber.

Or from literature:

The mystifying Sherlock Holmes.
The inventive Edward Lear.
The inspiring J. K. Rowling.
The noble Brontés.
The masterful Morpurgo.

Lesson Fifty-Seven: All-cheering sun

In *Romeo and Juliet* epithets are often applied to nature: in 1.1, there's the 'worshipped sun' (l.119) and the 'all-cheering sun' (l.134). In the same scene there's 'saint-seducing gold' (l.219). In 1.2 there's 'well-apparelled April' and 'limping winter' in adjacent lines (27–28).

> Ask the children to supply epithets for various weathers, and for objects beyond the earth – for cloud formations for example (look out of the window!); for the way the snow falls; for the coldness of February mornings mixed with thin sunlight; for the day when rain persists from breakfast to bedtime; for the stifling heat of a July afternoon in a classroom; for planetary bodies in their various states, the full moon, the half moon, the new moon; for the sun in winter, for the massed stars on a clear night, or a sighting of a comet or the planet Venus; for natural forces ('pulling-down gravity') . . .

The first set here is from a class of eight-year-olds, and the second from a class one year older. I have inserted comments for some of the examples that the individual writers made as they gave the work to me: 'saucering tornado', among others, would be obscure otherwise:

The outrageous waves ('they are going to cause a tsunami'); the rumbling roots ('in an earthquake'); the saucering tornado ('the way it picks things up'); the spiteful, heart-cracking hailstones; the body-blowing wind; the skin-ripping sun; the people cowering lightning; the everlasting darkness ('that's when you think winter will never end'); the majestic rainbow; the magnificent, mysterious rainbow; the soft-touching snow; the cold-blooded winter.

The nose-blocking winter; the claustrophobic winter ('when you can't go out at all'); the death-giving wave; the ear-bleeding thunder; the bull-charging thunder; the invisible faint wind; the pushing wind; the dancing wind; the hypnotising rainbow ('you have to look at it'); the suspicious rainbow; the bulleting rain; the igloo-making snow; the head-ripping, umbrella-piercing hailstones; the heart-whipping lightening; the death-giving wave; the relaxing wave.

And, finally, 'the infinite blue skies'.
Illustrating a phrase helps the children to get a firmer grip on its meaning.

> Ask the children to choose one epithet from the play, and to illustrate it in drawing or painting or in some other medium. Or ask them to draw or paint a costume for 'the fiery Tybalt'. It must be for a modern-dress production. How will the shapes and colours in the clothes suggest a man with a 'fiery' temper?

A word about puns. Some children understand them, but many do not. I have written about some of Shakespeare's examples in Note H.

Lesson Fifty-Eight: A rose by any other name – Phrases from the play that are still in use today

In the introduction, I pointed out how many of the plays are relevant to life today in major ways – *Hamlet*'s relevance in tyrannies everywhere, for example. In contrast, one minor measure of the extent to which Shakespeare's words have staying power is the frequency of his invented phrases that survive in everyday speech. All the following are, to a greater or lesser extent, still on English-speaking lips today.

> Divide the class into five groups, one for each act, and set them the task of finding these phrases. They should note their context, and write a sentence for each one in modern language. I have put an example after four of the following phrases given to me by a class of eleven-year-olds:

- star-crossed lovers (boyfriend and girlfriend who will never be together)
- parting is such sweet sorrow
- light of heart (happy as a feather is light)
- a fool's paradise
- what's in a name? (what does it matter what he is called?)
- a rose by any other name would smell as sweet
- cock-a-hoop (over the moon)
- as gentle as a lamb
- on a wild-goose chase
- on pain of death

- the weakest go to the wall

- go like lightning

- a plague on both your houses

- above compare

- what must be shall be

- I will not budge

- let me alone

- past help.

11 The Prologue, invitations to a party, and an angry prince

The Prologue

One way into the Prologue is to introduce the modern idea of a 'spoiler': the Prologue breaks a rule. It's not a rule about poetry – these fourteen lines make up a standard Shakespearean sonnet (see Note I) – it's a rule about story-telling. In Anne Fine's book *Bill's New Frock*, familiar to most primary age children, a boy wakes up and his mother gives him his new dress. When I first read the first page of this novel, I checked how many more pages the book had: when will I find out how this disturbing situation is resolved?

There is almost always that tension in a story. When we first pick up *Treasure Island*, we don't want to be told how John Silver turns out. We want to live with uncertainty, anticipating, not just the ending, but the delight we'll feel when all is resolved. Even though I re-read *Pride and Prejudice* every few years, I envy the teenager I was when I first read it, ignorant of the shame Lydia brings on her family, ignorant of how the Bennet family is rescued, ignorant (above all) of whether Elizabeth will marry Darcy.

Picture books, children's fiction, novels by Jane Austen or Catherine Cookson, modern plays, soap operas, police procedurals, drama, even sitcoms, romantic comedies – nearly of these obey this rule that is broken here.

Lesson Fifty-Nine: Spoiler alert! I

> Ask the children: when you begin to read a story, or see it on film, do you want to be told how it ends?
>
> Discuss all this with the children. How would they feel if their clever teenage big sister or brother told them how *Bill's New Frock* ends? Bring into the discussion a children's film currently showing. Would they want to know how it ends before they saw it?
>
> Ask the children to study the sonnet/Prologue carefully and make a note of all the words that suggest that a less-than-happy ending may be on its way. I think it is best if they do this in three stages: individually, then in small groups and finally as a class. In the course of this process, many ideas will be aired and discovered.
>
> Then they should ask: what story-telling rule has been broken here?

The Prologue is what is called today a 'spoiler'. Anne Fine might as well have written, after her first paragraph, a sentence telling us, Don't worry about Bill, this story will have a happy ending. The clues in the sonnet are easy to find. They are in lines 5–9: words like 'fatal', 'star-crossed', 'misadventured', 'death' and 'death-marked' give everything away. 'Grudge', 'mutiny', 'blood' and 'unclean' do not bode well either.

Of course, the term 'spoiler' is an anachronism, and the idea of suspense would have been unknown to Shakespeare and his contemporaries. But studying the Prologue in this way ensures that the children, at the very least, read it closely.

Lesson Sixty: Spoiler alert! II

Ask the children to write a trailer for this play that doesn't give away the end: perhaps they need to find questions rather than statements. It must tell the audience something about the play, it must make the play sound inviting, it must make them want to stay and watch. The trailer could be for any film about 'star-crossed lovers'. Some examples are:

'They meet. They love. Can all be well?

They are from different sides of town. Different places. Their skins are of a different colour. Can they ever love?

Her father, his father, her grandfather, his grandfather – for generations back these families have hated each other. Can these two ever be friends? Or even lovers . . .

This play is about a feud a hundred years old. And two innocent young people.

There are deaths in broad daylight in a high street. Where will they lead?

Should a father insist on choosing a husband for his only daughter?'

Lesson Sixty-One: The fisher with his pencil and the painter with his nets

Often minor characters have their moments in Shakespeare where an actor can briefly shine. Frequently, these parts were written for clowns, and it's often the darkest plays that have the funniest clowns. Three examples are the gravediggers in *Hamlet,* the Fool in *King Lear,* and the Porter in *Macbeth.* These men (always men) offset the tragedy that is the main story. In this play, there's one minor example from 1.2.38 onwards. I'm introducing him here before we find ourselves in the darker atmosphere the Prince's speech provides (see Lesson Sixty-Three).

Juliet's father, Lord Capulet, has sent his servant to deliver invitations to a party – the party, in fact, where Romeo and Juliet will meet. He gives two opportunities for comic business, one straight after the other. He can't read, and he muddles up workers and their tools:

SERVANT Find out them whose names are written here! It is written that the shoemaker should meddle with his yard and the tailor with his last, the fisher with his pencil, and the painter with his nets . . .

Define 'meddle' ('work with', 'deal with' in this context), 'yard' and 'last'. Ask the children to practice saying these lines in pairs. They could make the Servant sound stupid, or, more subtly, they could make him clever and merely pretending to be stupid. They should then write their own similarly muddled lines. This is a relatively easy activity, and one that everyone should be able to contribute to quite readily.

I collected these examples from a class of eight-year-olds:

A policeman with his Bible
A physiotherapist with her hammer

A palaeontologist with his cucumber
A chef with his dinosaur bone

A poet with his bus
A bricklayer with his wooden
spoon
A dog-trainer with his hi-vis
jacket
A butcher with his hose
A vicar with his earplugs
A cowboy with his cement-mixer
A bus driver with his tutu

A lollipop lady with lots of
money
An accountant with a lollipop
A musician with her red pen
A deep sea diver with a fire
truck
A secret agent with his
Easter egg
A poet with a canoe

Some of these leave a genuinely surreal impression: 'A palaeontologist with his cucumber', for example; others are straight out of a broad comedy tradition: 'A physiotherapist with her hammer' could be from a *Carry On* film (a series of cheap comedies from the 1960s and 1970s that relied entirely on innuendo and slapstick). On the other hand, there probably are policemen rarely separated from their Bibles, bus drivers who write poetry and vicars who use earplugs.

Lesson Sixty-Two: Signior Martino and his wife and daughters

Then Romeo reads the list of invitations that Capulet's servant is supposed to be delivering:

Signior Martino and his wife and daughters,
County Anselme and his beauteous sisters,
The lady widow of Vitruvio,
Signior Placentio and his lovely nieces,
Mercutio and his brother Valentine,
Mine uncle Capulet, his wife and daughters,
My fair niece Rosaline, and Lydia,
Signior Valentio and his cousin Tybalt,
Lucio and the lively Helena.

> There are at least two ways in which these lines could be read: soberly and practically, with Romeo simply helping the man out; or satirically. I think that the latter option is the more productive one. Emphasise adjectives like 'beautious', 'lovely' and 'lively'. Try to suggest empty-headed aristocracy with the words denoting rank, 'Signior' and 'County' (Count). Exaggerate pauses, perhaps, trying to sound like a senior footman announcing guests to a party in a costume drama. Then ask the children: Who would they like to make fun out of? Suggest that they choose public figures from any field of human life, including fiction, films and television.

I love the way the comic and the tragic, the fictional and the historical, the domestic and the political, the trivial and the serious all huddle and bustle in these lines. And there are those occasional shouts from the abstract ('punctuation and its catastrophic connectives'); the inanimate ('doors and their slamming qualities'); and then the plain daft. It was gratifying that the children had broken the boundaries which I had set:

Margaret Thatcher and her 8 million pound funeral,
Kelly Oleson from The Little House on the Prairie,
Goldilocks and her three fat bears,
Punctuation and its catastrophic connectives,
Kim Kardashian and her hippo posterior,
Doors and their slamming qualities,
My brother Ryan and his theft of my stuffed animals,
Microbes and their disastrous diseases,
The walrus and the carpenter and their big tummies,
The Sandy Hook shooter and his taken souls,
Monty Burns and his uranium,
Osama Bin Laden and how he killed my mom's best friend,
Cristina Kirchner for stealing our Nutella pots.

Incidentally, Romeo discovers from reading out this list that his beloved Rosaline will be at the party. How does he say her name? How does his delivery of the speech change gear at this point?

Lesson Sixty-Three: Neighbour-stained steel

Many of those ideas are light-hearted, but it is time to look at evidence of a dark central theme of the play – quarrelling. There are so many fights and arguments, and it is worth alerting children to this at the outset. There's the fight at the beginning (1.1) that leads to the confrontation between Tybalt and Mercutio; Tybalt's fury with Capulet (1.5); Mercutio's description of the quarrelsome Benvolio (3.1); the fatal duels between Mercutio and Tybalt and then Romeo and Tybalt (3.1); the terrible shouting of Capulet at his daughter (3.5). As the Friar warns Romeo, in a line that it serves the children well if they get it by heart, 'These violent delights have violent ends'. It's clear from this summary that Mercutio figures prominently in this context of violence. Indeed, he demanded a whole chapter to himself (Chapter 12)

At 1.1.72, the brawl at the beginning of the play between the servants of each house is ended by the prince's officers – the police – and then by the prince himself. Act these lines as dramatically as you can, shouting the first line; speaking 'Will they not hear?' to your servants beside you; emphasising, with actions perhaps (or even props) the violent words, especially 'steel', 'rage', 'torture'. You could have percussion of some kind banging and clashing until it gradually fades away around 'you beasts!'

> Rebellious subjects, enemies to peace,
> Profaner of this neighbour-stained steel –
> Will they not hear? – What ho, you men, you beasts!
> That quench the fire of your pernicious rage
> With purple fountains issuing from your veins:
> On pain of torture, from these bloody hands
> Throw your mistempered weapons to the ground,
> And hear the sentence of your moved prince . . .
> . . .
> . . . on pain of death, all men depart.

Discuss: what does 'neighbour-stained' mean? What are the 'purple fountains'? Explain 'pernicious'. By 'mistempered', the prince means 'made [tempered] for a wicked purpose'.

Ask the children to count the syllables in each line. There are almost always ten. Then ask the children to write their speeches for the prince, aiming to use lines of roughly the same length. These examples are from the apprentices, and they are full of violence inventively depicted: 'tubes of death', 'cords, triggers or muscles', 'wounds, drip, drip-staining the once grey pavement':

Hold it right there you forever fighting babies,
Drop your uncontrollable weapons to the ground.
I have a very important message.
If you raise these tubes of death again
You will be banished from this kingdom.
Now please create a path for me through this blood and gore
For I must be gone.
I cannot stand this or do much more.

Lottie

No more cords, triggers or muscles to be pulled,
Silence! – Do you not hear me? – I am talking! – Silence!
Your sentence, permanent death from me,
Your wounds, drip, drip-staining the once grey pavement,
Fast drip, drip, but slow, a hose left on,
Flooding the pavement with anger and sorrow,
Leave your weapons on the ground but go.
Leave! Leave! Leave! I will repeat. Leave!
And go home.

Anon.

Lesson Sixty-Four: Clubs, bills and partisans

Children should get used to that central theme of quarrelling early on in their understanding of this play. This lesson gives the children a chance to see how pervasive this fighting and feuding is in each of the five acts: we are never far from blows.

> Ask the children to find all mentions of the word 'quarrel' or connected ones: insulting words such as 'villain', words that seem intended to provoke a quarrel, words denoting weapons, words of violence. They should concentrate on the following scenes: Prologue, 1.1, 1.5, 2.4 (mostly the early part), 2.6, 3.1, 4.3 (Juliet's long speech) and 5.3. They should come up with these at least in 1.1:
>
> > 'quarrel' (at least three times), 'fought', 'weapon' (an obscene pun, of course, in 1.1.29), 'washing blow' (a slashing strike with the dagger), sword (at least four times), 'have at thee', 'clubs, bills and partisans' (all weapons), 'strike', 'beat', 'neighbour-stained steel', 'rage', 'purple fountains', 'torture', 'brawls', 'hate' . . .
>
> And those come from the first ninety-four lines, a mere three pages of script in the Cambridge School shakespeare edition. Early in 2.4, they should find 'torments', 'challenge', 'dead', 'stabbed', 'run through', 'fights', 'butcher', 'duellist', 'passado', 'punto reverso', 'hay' (the last three are fencing terms) and 'blade'.
>
> They should then write violent sentences of their own, finding modern words that try to match the feeling in Shakespeare's. To begin this activity, they might brainstorm in groups any modern words to do with quarrelling, fighting and warfare. Before they started, I read one class these lines in Mercutio's Queen Mab speech (Chapter 12):
>
> > . . . dreams he of cutting foreign throats,
> > Of breaches, ambuscados, Spanish blades . . . [see Chapter 12]
> > > 1.4.53–84

I collected these sentences from a class of ten-year-olds. They had been studying World War II. The classroom walls were covered with photographs of London during the Blitz, and earlier in the year they had also been introduced to some of Wilfred Owen's poetry about World War I. TV images of the civil war in Syria were also in their minds, I think. Because of all this influence, their writing was about warfare rather than personal fighting:

The doodlebugs whine in the night sky aiming death at the people . . . the bombs come down at night while the people are sleeping . . . fire bombs have torn the people's lives in pieces . . .

The city is nothing now but broken buildings with no roofs and smoke . . . Men in helmets charge against innocent people with their guns pointing at them, they want to kill, kill . . .

There is gleaming steel at the ends of all the soldiers' guns . . . Gas is in the air . . . bayonets and fire-shooting cannons . . .

12 'This is that very Mab'
Mercutio

Mercutio casts a spell stronger than any other character in the play (see Note J for more on this). In this first lesson, here is the comedian.

Lesson Sixty-Five: Thy head is full of quarrels

In 3.1.15–26, just before his fatal fight with Tybalt, Mercutio accuses Benvolio of being always ready to quarrel. In modern speech, he's 'winding him up'. It's a speech in prose of glorious silliness, because we already know that Benvolio tends toward the law-abiding: 'I do but keep the peace. Put up thy sword' he has said to Tybalt at 1.1.59. But Mercutio pretends to know better:

> Thou? why thou wilt quarrel with a man that hath a hair more or less in his beard than thou hast; thou wilt quarrel with a man for cracking nuts, having no other reason but because thou hast hazel eyes. What eye but such an eye would spy out such a quarrel? Thy head is as full of quarrels as a head is full of meat, and thy head has been beaten as addle as an egg for quarrelling. Thou hast quarreled with a man for coughing in the street, because he hath wakened thy dog that hath lain asleep in the sun. Didst thou not fall out with a tailor for wearing his new doublet before Easter? with another for tying his new shoes with an old riband? and yet thou wilt tutor me from quarrelling?

Rehearse the lines a few times so that you can speak them quickly. Then explain that an addled egg is a rotten one, that a doublet is a jacket and that (so I assume) the first tailor that Mercutio mentions shouldn't have been wearing a new jacket during the solemn Christian period of Lent. Then read this speech to the children. You might walk around the room, acting the picking of a quarrel with each child, pointing at him or her as you get to each opening 'Thou' and each new sentence. It is important that the children understand the essential humour of the speech: it is there, in part, to heighten the shock of the tragedy that is to occur within eighty lines – the funnier this speech is, the greater will be the impact of the killing. And it is not difficult to make it very funny.

Then discuss the absurdity of it – to quarrel because someone has more or fewer hairs in his beard than you have! Or because someone is cracking hazel nuts and you've got hazel eyes! Or because someone has woken your dog!

Then I ask them to bring it up to date, and to write a speech full of silly reasons for a quarrel. You will find that the children need some variation in the verbs, so now I collect synonyms for 'quarrel' before the children start. The thesaurus will offer verbs such as 'bicker', 'squabble', 'dispute', and 'scuffle'. As so often, it is a good idea for the children to spend time talking about modern words connected with quarrelling before they write their sentences down – and it is not always necessary for you to be in charge of each group as it works: trust them to generate words without your help. The more often you do this, the more trust in them you show, the better the results will be.

These examples come from the apprentices. I found that the staccato movement of Mercutio's speech (which I hadn't mentioned explicitly – it is a fallacy that what can be learnt must be taught) had crept in this first writer's piece. She had also introduced other elements into her writing – a morbid eccentricity, strange reading habits, gullibility:

You're the person who would quarrel with your dead cat just because it slept on your bed. You strange person, wearing black ever since it died – ten years ago. Why do you always read fairy tales, and not poems, scripts and autobiographies? What's got into you? You never, never use black pens because it reminds you of your cat, yet you wear black! Ever since I've known you, you always pick a fight, why don't you get a life and stop squabbling and be a normal civilised human being? You run to your mum when you're sad, you listen to people who tell you rubbish and believe them. But believe me, I only want to make you a better person, rather than a . . . a dead cat! You would bicker with someone who isn't even alive.

Lottie

The other writer is the youngest in the group, only a year away from her infant school. She achieves a delightful ending to her writing:

> You'll quarrel with a seamstress for selling pink ribbon to an innocent young girl. You'll argue with a fruit bowl for not having any English apples. You'll quarrel with Michael Jackson for being dead. You'll bicker with slugs for not having shells. You'll object to a tomato for not having any seeds. You'll argue with cracked slabs of concrete for not being fixed and with an ear-ring for not being a stud and with silver for not being gold. You'll quarrel with anything for not being everything.
>
> Evie

That is Mercutio the teasing joker. Now we see him as a dreamer and a poet, a conjurer of fanciful images from his own brain.

Lesson Sixty-Six: Queen Mab I

At 1.4.53–84 we find Mercutio explaining Romeo's love-sickness, at least to his own satisfaction:

O then I see Queen Mab hath been with you:
She is the fairies' midwife, and she comes
In shape no bigger than an agate stone
On the forefinger of an alderman,
Drawn with a team of little atomi
Over men's noses as they lie asleep.
Her chariot is an empty hazel-nut,
Made by the joiner squirrel or old grub,
Time out a'mind the fairies' coachmakers:
Her wagon spokes made of long spinners' legs,
The cover of the wings of grasshoppers,
Her traces of the smallest spider web,
Her collars of the moonshine's watr'y breams,
Her whip of cricket's bone, the lash of film,
Her waggoner, a small grey-coated gnat
Not half so big as a round little worm
Pricked from the lazy finger of a maid.
And in this state she gallops night by night
Through lovers' brains, and then they dream of love,
Oe'r courtiers' knees, that dream on cur'sies straight,
O'er lawyers' fingers, who straight dream on fees,
O'er ladies' lips, who straight on kisses dream

. . .

Sometime she driveth o'er a soldier's neck,
And then dreams he of cutting foreign throats,
Of breaches, ambuscadoes, Spanish blades . . .

In many of the activities in this book, I have made a virtue of how relatively straightforward they are to prepare and teach. This one is not like that. But if you are an enthusiast for Shakespeare's language, children's learning and the combustible potential when that language and that learning mix, the extra preparation required here is more than worth it. I have met teenagers who have remembered their experience of writing in the grip of this speech. Introducing children to Shakespeare in a way that causes them to interact with his poetry – to make it theirs – is to give some of them a present for life.

Before reading the Queen Mab speech to children, emphasise, first, the smallness of creatures and objects described: 'agate stone . . . forefinger . . . little atomi . . . empty hazel-nut . . . the smallest spider web . . . grasshoppers . . . cricket's bone . . . gnat'; and second, how it is concerned with nature. Explain some of the words. But it is best to make a virtue of the obscurity of some of them, rather than to go over each one meticulously: act, if you can, the preciousness of 'agate', caressing a ring of your own perhaps; act the tininess of the creatures that are named with hand gestures and a small voice; and act (easier, this one) the violence of the soldier's dreams. Then tell them the following:

- An agate is a semiprecious stone
- An alderman is a local politician
- Atomi (not quite as miniscule as our atoms, but getting on that way) are tiny creatures
- Courtiers are politicians, like aldermen, but more aristocratic, anxious for favour from kings and queens and dukes and duchesses and the like.

In the line 'Of breaches, ambuscadoes, Spanish blades', the children should, with minimal guidance, be able to infer the meanings of the words.

The speech is in two parts. The first part (ll.54–70) describes Mab's carriage, and the second (l.71 onwards) expresses Mercutio's belief, or rather his wild fantasy, that each human being dreams (thanks to Queen Mab) about their ambitions. Lawyers dream about money ('fees'), ladies about kisses, and soldiers about military triumphs.

Ask the children to choose one or two consecutive lines, and to write their own version of them.

I collected these examples from various schools:

She brings fairies' babies into the world.
She is as small as a jewel on a golden ring.

DJ

She rides over boyfriends' thoughts, and they dream of their girlfriends,
She rides over headmaster's hands and they dream about test results

Fatima

Sometimes she walks on soldier's fists, where they hold their grenades and their pistols and then they have nightmares . . .
Her reins are made of caterpillars' legs and her driver is a fly.

Brian

Lesson Sixty-Seven: Queen Mab II

I sometimes use that last activity – using short sections of Mercutio's Queen Mab speech – as a practice for the next activity, much as a cricketer uses the practising of a stroke in the nets for his main job, the scoring of runs in a match. But sometimes I don't bother with the small sections of the speech. When we are with children we know well; in whom we have confidence, and confidence in our own relationship with them; when we have a passion, or something approaching a passion for Shakespeare's words . . . then we can be more ambitious. And we can ask the children to write their own Queen Mab speeches.

> Read the speech again. Then ask the children to be wild, as fanciful as Mercutio. He is using his imagination, and they must follow his example: almost anything goes! They might bring in any dreamers and, indeed, any dreams. Or any nightmares.

First, these examples are extracts from writing by children identified as a set of the most capable writers in a year of ten-year-olds:

O then I see Queen Mab hath been with you –

creaking over the singer's throat
thinking about acting and singing and stress,
dancing across Kate Middleton's head,
thinking about impressing the Queen with elegance and grace.
O then I see Queen Mab hath been with you.

Vidushi

*She rides over an inspector, going over his eyes to get evidence
about the school.
She rides over the headteacher's brain making him dream about a
wonderful school.
She rides over the children's heads so they dream about hearing
the test results.
She rides over an owl's beak making him think about scrumptious
beetles.
She rides over a shark's eyes making him dream about a million
and one seals to gobble.
She rides over a lion's legs to make him dream about chasing and
digesting a deer.*

Bubbly

*She rides on Merlin's eyes
And makes him dream of a magic Camelot
With no evil anywhere.
She rides on Robin Hood's hands
And makes him dream of riches
And no such thing as poverty.
She rides on Tarzan's body
And makes him dream of cleanliness.*

Huzaifa

These children, on the other hand, are members of a mixed-ability class of
ten-year-olds:

O then I see Queen Mab hath been with you –

*She is the fairy queen's messenger
No bigger than a warm teardrop rolling down a young lady's face,
Her chariot pulled by three moths with brown wings.
The wheels are made of miniscule blades of grass,*

The roof is a flattened caterpillar's chrysalis . . .
She rides across athletes' foreheads and makes them dream of
winning competitions — oh the pride! Oh the glory!
She rides over giant hills, formerly known as noses,
Noses of chefs making them dream of getting a five star review on
their 'asparagus risotto' . . .

Jenny

You have King Mab's spell on you.
He gets around in an acorn shell
And his reins are as thin as spider's silk.
He is the size of a daisy petal
Trying to stand out to all the other petals.
He makes people dream of England winning the 2014 World Cup
In Rio de Janero, Brazil.
His eyes are as small as a one-centimetre pebble
And his lips are as pale as a dead rose petal.
He can flutter like a butterfly drifting around in the scorching
heat.

Luke

Lesson Sixty-Eight: Queen Mab III

> Tell the children to imagine that they have been asked to produce a small play based on Mercutio's speech. The first job is to design Queen Mab's chariot. Remind them of some of the lines: the 'empty hazel-nut', the 'waggon-spokes' made of 'spinners' legs', the 'cover of the wings of grasshoppers', the 'traces' (reins) of 'the smallest spider web' and so on. They should make their chariots from tiny natural objects, like Mercutio's. They should then write on their drawings either a line from Mercutio's speech that is appropriate to it, or a line of their own. Or both.

And here is a related activity:

> Revise some of Mercutio's lines in the previous lessons. Ask the children to brainstorm in groups the adjectives that describe his personality. Then share their words in class. Ask them to design a costume for the character. You might ask them to work in pairs, with both children making suggestions, and one doing the drawing, while the other continues to make suggestions. The point of this activity is not so much the act of drawing, but the talk that the children engage in, thereby exploring the character and furthering each other's understanding of him.

Figure 12.1 Mercutio, by Ellie Barker

Lesson Sixty-Nine: Prince of Cats

That is what Mercutio calls Tybalt when describing him to Benvolio at 2.4.18–24. He continues:

> O, he's the courageous captain of compliments: he fights as you sing prick-song, keeps time, distance, and proportion; he rests his minim rests, one, two, and a third in your bosom; the very butcher of a silk button, a duellist, a duellist; a gentleman of the very first house, of the first and second cause. Ah, the immortal 'passado', the 'punto reverso', the 'hay'!

Explain some of the words: 'Tybalt' was a popular name for a cat – but, even more to the point, 'cat' says something about the sharpness of Tybalt's weapons. 'Prick-song' was printed music: Mercutio goes on to compare Tybalt's precise fighting style to music, both being governed by strict rules. 'Passado' is a lunge, 'punto reverso' a back-handed thrust, 'hay' meant 'hit'. I am grateful to Gibson's edition of the play (1992) for this information.

Ask the children to write a description of a man or woman today who is always spoiling for a fight. They should decide what kind of fighter first: someone who comes in fists flailing, a brawler; a precise and deadly fighter, like Tybalt; a user of knives, or just fists; a fierce-tempered fighter; a clinical calm one; a fighter with words as well as physical actions; a sneaky, cunning fighter.

Lesson Seventy: A plague a' both your houses!

The purpose of this lesson is to give children a glimpse of early Shakespeare at its most dramatic. At 3.1.70–83, Mercutio has been wounded by Tybalt, who rushes away with his friends. The children should imagine a street brawl here. Mercutio gasps:

I am hurt.
A plague a' both your houses! I am sped.
Is he gone and hath nothing?

. . .

Ay, ay, a scratch, a scratch, marry, 'tis enough.
Where is my page? Go, villain, fetch a surgeon.

. . .

No, 'tis not so deep as a well, nor so wide as a church-door, but 'tis enough, 'twill serve. Ask for me tomorrow, and you shall find me a grave man. I am peppered, I warrant, for this world. A plague 'a both your houses! 'Zounds, a dog, a rat, a mouse, a cat, to scratch a man to death! a braggart, a rogue, a villain, that fights by the book of arithmetic. Why the dev'l came you between us? I was hurt under your arm.

. . .

Help me into some house, Benvolio,
Or I shall faint. A plague 'a both your houses!
They have made worms' meat of me. I have it,
And soundly too. Your houses!

This is one of the most dramatic deaths in Shakespeare. In just thirteen lines! Tybalt and Mercutio fence, Romeo intervenes, and Tybalt wounds Mercutio fatally.

The lines above are some of Mercutio's last words.

> Say these words to the class as truthfully as you can. I mean by this, do what the script tells you to do. Notice how Mercutio begins and ends speaking verse, but has a section in prose. Notice his bitterness – in that pun on 'grave', in his curse on the Capulets and the Montagues, in the sarcastic understatement, in his description of his wound; notice how he still has breath and time to regret that Tybalt has escaped unwounded. His last two words, 'Your houses!' are his pathetic attempt to repeat his earlier curse.
>
> As you prepare, notice the punctuation: treat the commas as coded stage directions. For example, Mercutio struggles for breath at each comma in the lines 'a dog, a rat, a mouse, a cat, to scratch a man to death! a braggart, a rogue, a villain, that fights by the book of arithmetic.' Or possibly, he is looking in horror at what he glimpses behind his palm, as he peeps under it, forgetting its main need, to stem the gush of blood: 'not so deep as a well, nor so wide as a church-door, but 'tis enough . . .'
>
> Or it's both! His breath is going, but he must look . . . And the short phrases that tend to shorten as the lines proceed have the same function: Mercutio's body is failing him by the moment.
>
> It is not hard to act that with voice alone.

Ask the children for more epithets about Mercutio, this time as he lies dying:

life-drained, soul-drained, hope-lost, breath-struggling, life-gasping, speech-struggling, eternally lost, shutting down, death-maddened, hollow, battery-drained

non-rechargeable

[these last two from the same straight-faced child].

13 'O love is handsome'
Romeo and Juliet

Romeo's personality looks pale when set close to Mercutio's (see Note J for reasons for this judgement). Juliet, even though she is younger than her lover, is more mature than him, and has the more dramatic lines, especially in her long soliloquy at the beginning of 4.3. The pentameter that begins it at line 15 is frightening in its monosyllabic simplicity, its physicality ('veins') and its strange use of 'thrills' as a verb: 'I have a faint cold fear thrills through my veins'. Children are appalled at her fear of being buried alive; her fear that she might

> . . . pluck the mangled Tybalt from his shroud,
> And in this rage, with some great kinsman's bone,
> As with a club, dash out my desp'rate brains . . .

Bracing. So let's begin this chapter with Juliet.

Lesson Seventy-One: A faint cold fear

There are times when I wouldn't teach this lesson in a primary school: if I didn't know the children, for example; if I knew there were children with chronic emotional difficulties present; or if I didn't have the support of the class teacher. Nevertheless, getting to know the play means visiting, at least once, its darkest places. And art has a function in preparing us for the dark places where we will find ourselves at one time or another.

Well, here we go.

 Read these lines to the children:

I have a faint cold fear thrills through my veins
That almost freezes up the heat of life . . .

as well as any other lines you feel like reading from the speech. Then ask them to write lines in which they try to convey something of the same mood. Note that most adults would balk at such a suggestion – I would never suggest it to teachers on one of my Inset writing courses – but many children, on the other hand, dive in with what looks like reckless enthusiasm.

A hiding frozen death is in my veins.
Evan

Silently the terror poisons me.
There is a freezing chill running through hell.
Ayesha

A new hot horror surges through my blood.
                                        Xavier

Hot worry pulls at my thumping heart.
                                        Ellie

Some people, I know, may not like to believe it, but children probably think about the terrors of the unknown daily. Such thinking might follow deaths in the family. It may be a consequence, unintended or otherwise, of certain kinds of religious upbringings. In any case, it will probably be shapeless, and therefore frightening. Offering children opportunities to write about these terrors helps them to shape their fears into objects made up of words, and then those fears can be contemplated with greater equanimity. It is healthier to reflect on death, for example, through the medium of writing, than it is to lie in bed worrying about it.

Lesson Seventy-Two: Give me my Romeo

But here is the essence of the play's love theme. It's Juliet in ecstasy at 3.2.21–25, minutes before the Nurse, her servant who has known her since she was born, tells her that Romeo has killed her cousin Tybalt:

Give me my Romeo, and when I shall die,
Take him and cut him out in little stars,
And he will make the face of heaven so fine
That all the world will be in love with night,
And pay no worship to the garish sun.

 Read these lines to the children. Ask them to identify the starry metaphor that Juliet is using and then ask them simply to imitate this speech.

The following examples are by the apprentices:

Burn me on a camp fire in winter.
Throw my ashes into the trees
So my scent will always exist.
                              Evan

You are my moonlit river bank,
My twinkling stars,
My shimmering sun.
When it is snowing
You are my pearl necklace which I will wear in my darkest hour.
                              Ellie

Lesson Seventy-Three: Mistress minion

This lesson is about Juliet and her father's fury in 3.5. Juliet has married Romeo in secret with the help of Friar Lawrence. Now, unaware of this, of course, her father has decided she will marry his chosen suitor, the Count Paris, who is a much better prospect from his point of view: he has a title and, much more than that, he is not a Montague. This is to be an arranged marriage, a phrase that still resonates with some children's lives today.

Now, to put it mildly, Juliet has a twofold problem. First, she loves Romeo and feels nothing for Paris; and, second, bigamy is a mortal sin. It is worth emphasising this second point. The situation is not simply that of a wilful teenager and her angry father: to discuss it in such a way would be to belittle it. Any contemporary of Juliet's would have believed that, if she contracted a second marriage, she would go to hell. No wonder Juliet's mind has been dwelling on terrible things.

Here are some of Capulet's furious words in 3.5, with one of Juliet's responses:

CAPULET . . . mistress minion you . . .
. . . fettle your fine joints 'gainst Thursday next,
To go with Paris to Saint Peter's Church,
Or I will drag thee on a hurdle thither.
Out, you green-sickness carrion! out you baggage!
You tallow-face! . . .

. . .

JULIET Good father, I beseech you on my knees,
Hear me with patience but to speak a word.
CAPULET Hang thee, young baggage, disobedient wretch!
I tell thee what: get thee to church a 'Thursday,
Or never after look me in the face.
Speak not, reply not, do not answer me!

My fingers itch . . .

. . . Out on her, hilding!

> Read these lines with as much fury as you can act. You might arrange for a child to interject with Juliet's lines. Then explain some of the words. 'Minion' can simply mean 'child', but here is it spoken with venom; 'fettle' means 'get ready', but Capulet's phrase 'fettle your fine joints' refers to horses; 'hilding' means 'worthless person'. In the line 'Or I will drag thee on a hurdle thither', Capulet is saying that he will drag his daughter to church on a sledge. Underline what a humiliation for a young woman this would be.

The children should write speeches modelled on Capulet's:

FATHER You fool. You terrible child. You are more horrid than the generation of horridness. You shall never speak again.
DAUGHTER But my father –
FATHER Keep your mouth closed. And don't you dare 'but' me, who do you think you are?
DAUGHTER Well, I think I'm your –
FATHER What part of keep your mouth closed don't you get. I can see how guilty you are. It's in your eyes. You are a waste of time. You disobey me all through.
DAUGHTER Father you just understand that you have to forgive me sooner or later.

Melana

Melana, a girl in a mixed-ability class, wrote this the first time I taught this lesson. Much of the resulting work in this class used childish terms – 'twit' and the like – so when I approached these lines a week later with the apprentices, I was careful to sharpen the focus on the play's language, on the character of Capulet and his language in particular, and on adults and the way they might speak in a situation like this:

You animal savage contaminating our blood!
How dare you say such words to me under my roof?
All we do for you!
You useless lump of dirt to be swept away with a broom
from our noble home!
We offer you the best, Paris!
and now you ungrateful ... ungrateful ... ungrateful brick
you return it with this!
You are a waste of the food I put on your plate!
You bring disgrace on the whole family.
We were noble but now we're disgraceful.

Xavier

Is that how you thank me?
God knows why you were born!
Get out of my eyesight before hell reaches down and snatches you
up.
If I were you I'd build myself a grave saying
'I never proved to my father the living daughter he wanted'
and die there on the spot like rat.

Lottie

You never live up to my rather low standards.
You a waste of space,
you waste of skin,
you waste of the air you breathe.
You mucky puddle sitting lonely and stranded sitting next
to a cheerful happy river flowing down
like the long beautiful hair of Rapunzel's head.

Ayesha

Lesson Seventy-Four: Private in his chamber – Romeo

At the beginning of the play, the hero is lovesick over Rosaline, a girl we never see. Our first glimpse of him is through the eyes of his worried father in 1.1.122–131. There's been a brawl, the servants' street fight that is the lowlife pre-echo of what will happen with more drama and consequence later in 3.1 when Mercutio and Tybalt will die. Old Montague is telling Benvolio how his son often walks early in the day in a grove of sycamore trees:

> Many a morning hath he there been seen,
> With tears augmenting the fresh morning's dew,
> Adding to clouds more clouds with his deep sighs,
> But all so soon as the all-cheering sun
> Should in the farthest east begin to draw
> The shady curtains from Aurora's bed,
> Away from light steals home my heavy son,
> And private in his chamber pens himself,
> Shuts up his windows, locks fair daylight out,
> And make himself an artificial night . . .

This speech is in language typical of Shakespeare's early poetry, with its regular iambic pentameters (see Note I), its exaggerated comparisons ('clouds' with 'sighs', 'tears' with 'dew') and its classical reference. It is the kind of language that is all too easily parodied, and it may strike some of us as forced, but it has a formal beauty which comes from that stately rhythm and also from the frequency of the long vowel sounds: 'or' in 'morning', 'aug' in 'augmenting', 'draw', 'Aurora'; and the long 'i' sounds in 'sighs', 'light', 'private', 'daylight' and 'night'. Poor Montague represents fathers of adolescent boys down the ages. The love which counted for so much, which was so powerful, so uncomplicated and so requited when the boy was small, is now powerless as the son moves away from his father. Or at least it seems to be so. This speech enacts the restrained sadness in Montague's heart.

Read these lines to the children. Explain 'augmenting' (adding to) and 'Aurora' (dawn). Keep in mind, as you read, those long vowel sounds and the stately measured movement of the lines. Emphasise the repeated 'morning', 'clouds' and 'light' (one in 'daylight'), and important final rhyming word 'night'. You could also read the lines about the third of the seven ages of man from *As You Like It*: 'And then the lover, sighing like furnace, with a woeful ballad / Made to his mistress eyebrow' (2.7.139–167). They also describe the condition that afflicts Romeo.

Ask the children to talk among themselves about teenagers – brothers, sisters, cousins, neighbours, friends. How do they behave when they are moody for no reason anyone else can see? When they are simply sad?

Ask the children to write some lines inspired by Montague. They should write in lines of verse with ten syllables (or nine or eleven) in each line. You could share with them these lines written by a teacher during one of my lessons (printed here by permission):

The bedroom door's shut fast, and from behind it

Shouts a music made of violence, the thumps

And punches of a maddened anger, the yells

Of a being nothing to do with me

Yet one drawn years ago from deep inside me.

I walk down the long dark garden searching

For silence and for the child I once knew better

Than, it seemed, I knew myself . . .

One ten-year-old wrote about her older brother:

> Mood
> locks himself up
> only to stare at the ceiling
> gazes idly at a poster
> dreaming up a false picture.
>   Andrea

One ten-year-old told me about a friend of hers 'about thirteen, I think, we always used to play together, almost every day. Now he just stays in his room'. I love the way she has caught in the spareness of her lines the blank situation:

> Stand … wait … sigh
> it's all he ever does.
> I used to ask him what's the matter with him.
> Now, I don't bother.
> I'm never going to get a reply.
> Waiting for her.
> He'll do anything for her.
> If only the love was symmetrical.
> Are you okay?
> Grumble.
> Need anything?
> Mumble.
> Was it her?
> Sigh.
>
>   Ayesha

> Locked up in his hellish room,
> a frown is engraved on his grey face.
>   Ellie

Lesson Seventy-Five: A madness most discreet

The conventional view of *Romeo and Juliet* is that it's a play about love. Ask around randomly about it, and you will be given a literary amalgam of chocolate box, valentine card and sweet white wine. Of course, we know by now that it is a much more complicated and much richer business than that.

However, Romeo attempts a definition of love (as he is experiencing it with the distant Rosaline) at 1.1.181–185. Notice here that, once again, he can't resist oxymorons: 'A madness most discreet' (an oxymoronic kenning? – see below), 'loving tears':

Love is a smoke made with the fume of sighs,
Being purged, a fire sparkling in lovers' eyes,
Being vexed, a sea nourished with loving tears.
What is it else? A madness most discreet,
A choking gall, and a preserving sweet.

> Speak these lines to the class. You could toss kennings usefully into the mix. A kenning – the word comes from the Old Norse for 'know' or 'recognise' – is a way of naming something. It's common in Scandinavian and Anglo-Saxon verse: 'widow-maker' for 'sword' and 'whale-road' for 'sea' are two examples. 'Praise-bringer', 'hope-maker', 'death-bringer', 'bookmark of life', 'spark of togetherness' are examples of kennings about love in the work below. The apprentices had used Romeo's lines, but the kennings they'd played with recently enriched their writing.
>
> You could read, first, Romeo's lines, then the Viking kennings and finally, if it helps, some of the writing below.

These are by the apprentices:

> Love is the strongest force,
> the one that always makes it to first place,
> it's a praise-bringer, a hope-maker
> but
> also a death-bringer.
>
> > > Ellie

> Love is a deceiver
> a beast with no reason
> over in a heartbeat!
>
> > > Katie

> Love is an everlasting, unravelling poem.
>
> > > Savannah

> Love is a bookmark of life.
>
> > > Kai

> Love is like
> a deep fire.
> It's a spark of togetherness and
> a bullet of dependence.
> It's a locked up feeling
> which can now be set free
> and a garden of hope and trust and
> the F and G on a keyboard
> but in the end love is like
> a game of two cheaters.
>
> > > Lee

I don't know why love is 'F and G on a keyboard'.

Nine-year-olds in a multi-ethnic school in East London also wrote with Romeo's lines in mind. This time, I didn't mention kennings, but some turned up anyway:

Love is happiness, love is depression, love is frustration.
Noor

Love will sometimes cause problems and they are a plague
spreading to each other.
New lovers get excited,
old lovers only get half of the excitement.
When anger is down love is up.
When love is down anger is up.
Ruthya

Love is heat and cold bonding together with trust.
Bubbly

Love is romance but when love falls in tragedy it is just waste.
Ayat

Love is something that is a hard thing to express.
When love is old it feels like the ropes let go.
Rifa

The contributions of Ruthya ('New lovers get excited, old lovers only get half of the excitement') and Rifa, with her last line, remind me of an old folk song usually called 'O Waly Waly' that contains some of the saddest lines in the folk tradition: '. . . love's a jewel while it is new / But when it is old it groweth cold / And fades away like morning dew'. The presence of such sceptical understanding in children is a reminder that we all too often underrate what children have partial knowledge about, or more accurately, I think, have premonitions about. And we also underrate the power they have to hand to write about them. Indeed, nearly all the pieces have a steely edge of honesty; there's almost nothing of the Clinton Cards sentimentality I half-expected, and when it does emerge in the phrase 'garden of love and trust' its prettiness is immediately and violently undercut with 'a game of two cheaters'.

Lesson Seventy-Six: He that hath the steerage of my course

One curiosity about Romeo is that there is evidence in his words that he is religious. This is true in a vague sense: he believes in the stars, he often uses the word 'light' suggestively (for example, at 1.4.12: 'Give me a torch . . . / . . . I will bear the light', and later in the same scene, l.38: 'I'll be a candle-holder'). But many of his lines go further than that and make it clear that he is a devout Christian. This is unusual in Shakespeare – I can think of no other hero who uses words like those below. Perhaps they are in the play because they make vivid contrasts with the wild Mercutio and the fierce Tybalt.

> Arrange the children in groups, and ask them to go through these scenes and make notes of all words and phrases that have a broadly religious echo or, more specifically, a Christian one. They might also note all references to light and stars. The scenes are 1.2, 1.4, 1.5, 2.2, 2.3. You might prepare them by discussing with them definitions of these words: 'devout', 'heretic', 'holy', 'shrine' and others.

Here is a list of some of the religious references:

- In Act 1 there are these: at 1.2.88, Romeo refers to 'the devout religion of my eye'. In the same speech, he refers to 'heretics [being] burnt'. Children know that, in his time, heretics were indeed burnt for not accepting what was considered orthodox Christian belief. At 1.4.113, he says a prayer: 'But He that hath the steerage of my course /Direct my sail!'

- 1.5 needs special treatment! The lines beginning at l.92 with 'If I profane' to 'prayer's effect I take' must be the only mutual declaration of love in all English literature that uses twelve Christian or Christian-referring words: 'profane' (from the Latin *profanus* 'outside the temple', but 'anti-religious' in this context), 'holy' (twice), 'shrine', 'sin', 'pilgrims' (four times), 'devotion', 'saints' (three times), 'palmer', (= pilgrim, twice), 'prayer', 'pray', 'faith', 'despair' (a medieval sin, the opposite of faith). Eighteen usages, counting repeats. And that's in fourteen lines, a sonnet. When the sonnet is finished, both Romeo and Juliet refer to 'sin' five times, four with that word, and one with its synonym 'trespass'. You might quote here the prayer book words in the Lord's Prayer: 'Forgive us our trespasses . . .'

- 2.2 has 'vestal' at l.8 (this is not Christian, but comes from ancient Roman religion: vestal virgins were devotees of the goddess Diana); 'heaven' (l.15 and l.20); at 26–29, Romeo says: 'O speak again, bright angel, for thou art . . .// As is a winged messenger of heaven' (a definition of the word 'angel'); 'baptised' at l.50; 'saint' at l.55. At l.82, he seems to echo his earlier prayer about the steerage of his soul: 'I am no pilot, yet wert thou as far / As that vast shore washed with the farthest sea, / I should adventure . . .'

- 2.3.45 has 'my ghostly father'. This is a reference to the confession box, and the way in which the priest is hidden. Romeo clearly makes his confession to the Friar regularly. A few lines later, he refers to the Friar's help as 'holy physic' (medicine) and calls him 'blessed'. These two characters, as well as being priest and layman, are clearly close friends.

- Note that Juliet, in 3.5 at l.62 describes Romeo as someone 'That is renowned for faith'.

After the end of 2.3 Romeo's Christian references fade away. Ask the students: why might this be? Presumably because events have changed him: Mercutio's death, his killing of Tybalt and, above all, his falling in love with Juliet, have pushed his religion to one side.

 Now ask the children to focus on two of these lines:

But He that hath the steerage of my course
Direct my sail!

Read it and repeat it to the children. Ask them three questions. Emphasise that there are no definitive answers to the first two: Who do they think this 'He' is that Romeo is talking about? (God? The Lord? Allah? Nature?) What do they think a 'soul' might be? What is the metaphor that Romeo is using here? Then ask them to write their own Romeo-inspired prayers, using metaphors, but not ones to do with sailing.

Ten-year-olds, the first four from different religious traditions from Romeo, wrote their prayers, using metaphors from cookery, flight, music and, of all things, viniculture:

He that hath the power and strength of this fire guide me through it.

Mustafa

He that gives me emotion make it STRONGER!
He that has the control over my frying pan make me a better cook.
He that has control over my aircraft guide me through this war.

Bubbly

He that has control of my voice direct my music.

Aqib

He that has control of my spirit guide me to heaven.

Ayat

You who have the infinite fuel
turn the rolling wheels.

Ellie

He who flies my heart take me down safely.

Evan

He who manipulates my growing vine
send it upwards.

Ayesha

You could end this lesson by mentioning more references to light and associated words, all spoken by Romeo:

1.5.43: O she doth teach the torches to burn bright!

2.2.2 But soft, what light from yonder window breaks? / It is the east, and Juliet is the sun. Line 26 'bright angel'; line 155 'light'.

Lesson Seventy-Seven: A sonnet

See Note I for more on sonnets.

At 1.5.92–105, Romeo and Juliet have met and fallen in love. Speak their lines to each other. The first thing to convey, if possible, is the sheer magic of the situation, and the way the lines convey it through a kind of music. Emphasise in your reading:

- the gentleness of the consonants

- how the 'this/kiss' rhyme is repeated in the second four lines, breaking the usual sonnet rule, and thus emphasising the second word

- the frequent repetition of the syllables 'pray' and 'palm'

- how the moment before the kiss after l.14 is recorded with a rhyming couplet, with Juliet speaking the first rhyming line, and Romeo the second.

Then hand out copies and revise all the words in the sonnet that have religious connotations

ROMEO If I profane with my unworthiest hand
This holy shrine, the gentle sin is this,
My lips, two blushing pilgrims, ready stand
To smooth that rough touch with a tender kiss.

JULIET Good pilgrim, you do wrong your hand too much,
Which mannerly devotion shows in this;
For saints have hands that pilgrims' hands do touch,
And palm to palm is holy palmers' kiss.

ROMEO Have not saints lips, and holy palmers too?

JULIET Ay, pilgrim, lips that they must use in prayer.

ROMEO O, then, dear saint, let lips do what hands do:
They pray — grant thou, lest faith turn to despair.

JULIET   Saints do not move, though grant for prayers' sake.

ROMEO Then move not, while my prayer's effect I take.

Ask the children to look back at the Prologue at the beginning of the play. What do those fourteen lines have in common with these fourteen? Help the children to identify the number of the lines, the number of syllables in each line and the rhyme scheme.

Lesson Seventy-Eight: Canker death

The central characters die by their own hands in Juliet's tomb, and these deaths are prefigured by the deaths of Romeo's friend Mercutio and Juliet's cousin Tybalt. Indeed, it is true to say that *Romeo and Juliet* is about death as much as love.

Divide the class into five groups, with each group taking one act, with the Prologue included in Act 1 and the second chorus in Act 2. They should write down every use of a word associated with death, and its context. They should include words that are often, if not always, used in a death context, such as 'poison'. Here are my findings on 2.2 and 3.5:

- 2.3 yields the following: 'tomb' (l.9: the earth is nature's); 'burying grave' (in the next line: earth's womb is also her grave; 'stays all senses': l.26); 'canker death' (death is a growth that eats up living things); 'bury' (l.83: as a metaphor for ceasing to love); 'grave' (l.84; a frequent word in the play – the groups could combine to find exactly how frequent it is).

- 3.5 has these: 'die' (l.12); 'death' (l.16 and l.24); 'tomb' (l.36)' and 'dead' (l.56).

- And these related words (given the context): 'gone' (l.1, 11, 35, 43); 'dark' (twice in l.36); 'farewell' (twice at l.43, again at l.48); 'descend' (l.42).

Lesson Seventy-Nine: Epithets again

When the children have become familiar with the characters in the play, ask them to think hard for a few minutes about them. What is Romeo's personality? Juliet's? Capulet's? Revise the work on epithets in Chapter 10. Ask the children to make new epithets about these three. You could offer some of these to get them started. As usual, a thesaurus will help, but they should rack their brain first:

Capulet: raging, frightening, furious, violent; The Nurse: loud, rude, raucous, caring; Romeo: bewitched, easily-entranced; Juliet: brave, confused . . .

What epithets can the children find for Lord Capulet, the Friar and Paris?

14 'Strange eventful history'
Other passages from Shakespeare's work

There are a hundred-odd passages in other Shakespeare plays that can delight children and inspire good writing. The last part of this book is devoted to four of them. Two are of some length, one consists of a single line, and the last is the most famous of the sonnets. They all demand commitment on the part of teacher and student, and are probably best used when the children are familiar with some of the passages in the earlier chapters of my book.

Lesson Eighty: All the world's a stage

The first passage is one of the most famous speeches: scraps of some of the lines are at the back of many people's minds, even if they are not sure where they came from. 'All the world's a stage', for example; 'mewling and puking'; 'the whining schoolboy'. This speech is from *As You Like It*, 2.7.139–167, and is spoken by the melancholy Jacques:

> All the world's a stage,
> And all the men and women merely players;
> They have their exits and their entrances,
> And one man in his time plays many parts,
> His acts being seven ages. At first, the infant,
> Mewling and puking in the nurse's arms.
> Then the whining schoolboy, with his satchel
> And shining morning face, creeping like snail
> Unwillingly to school. And then the lover,
> Sighing like furnace, with a woeful ballad
> Made to his mistress' eyebrow. Then a soldier,
> Full of strange oaths and bearded like the pard,
> Jealous in honour, sudden and quick in quarrel,
> Seeking the bubble reputation
> Even in the cannon's mouth. And then the justice,
> In fair round belly with good capon lined,
> With eyes severe and beard of formal cut,
> Full of wise saws and modern instances;
> And so he plays his part. The sixth age shifts
> Into the lean and slippered pantaloon,

With spectacles on nose and pouch on side;
His youthful hose, well saved, a world too wide
For his shrunk shank, and his big manly voice,
Turning again toward childish treble, pipes
And whistles in his sound. Last scene of all,
That ends this strange eventful history,
Is second childishness and mere oblivion,
Sans teeth, sans eyes, sans taste, sans everything.

I've written this before: it is not necessary to explain every obscure word to children – often the context will help to make Shakespeare's meaning clear, and in any case, many children enjoy experiencing strange words. And with a little acting, we can suggest the meaning of 'mewling' and 'puking' (the use of the second of these, incidentally, is the first one recorded in the language). However, sometimes we might feel we need to explain some of the words. Here, 'pard' is 'leopard', a 'capon' is an edible cockerel (according to Onions' 1911 book, judges were often bribed with these birds, so the word has satirical intent); a 'saw' is a 'saying', 'oblivion' is 'forgetfulness', 'sans' (pronounced as if it were an English word) is French for 'without'. 'Shank' is an out-of-date word for 'leg' that survived until a few years ago in the phrase 'I'm going by Shanks's pony' – that is, I'm walking.

> Act this speech as best you can. Some of the ages are easy: the infant's puking, the schoolchild's school-wards trudge, the lover's sighing, the soldier's military bearing, the old folk at the end – none of these should present a problem. Then divide the children into seven groups, one for each age, and ask them to make up-to-date versions. I always suggest that, unless they actually know one, they swap the soldier for a young person in a first job – supermarket checkout, paper boy or girl, apprentice – student would work too. And they might swap the judge for another important person – headteacher, priest, politician, bank manger, doctor. All the characters, of course, can be of either sex.

The eleven- and twelve-year-old writers quoted below were taking part in a residential writing course. They'd been in the company of two writers, and had spent most of the daylight hours writing:

The baby crying, weeping for its rattle, pink and blue,
Whinging for a drop of warm milk ready from the microwave
but then when night falls, peace, quiet until …

Dribble coming from his mouth,
tearless crying, cradled lovingly,
passed around the room.

The schoolchild mopes mournfully to school
scuffing hated school shoes in despair
and turning up the road to imprisonment.

The schoolgirl being forced to enter lessons
Answering reluctantly the register
Secretly rolling up her skirt
Being shouted at: 'Skirt on the knee!'

He strolls up for his first job
feeling on top of the world,
voice booming, making everyone flinch.

The lovers, committed, connected on their wedding day
flirting along all night, all day,
growing too old, but will they stay
forever, forever till death us do part?

He sits, love-stricken, staring at the keyboard,
his hair flapping over his eyes,

clutching his arm, covering the heart with 'Amie' on it.
His excuse was 'She thinks tattoos are cool.'

The door-to-door salesman dragging his display case,
his crafty smile and pleasant convincing tone
as he flogs his goods to his unsuspecting victims.

The businessman, smartly dressed and ready for a day's work,
his schedule neatly typed, his meetings listed,
his desk neat and all his equipment organised.

The landlord of the pub calling for last orders again,
yelling Go away, it's closing time at last!
pushing the grumbling drunks out of the door.

Forever talking
ready to say it again
everyday a different task
diving into writing, a hobby expressed.
The old man sits in his dressing gown
Watching UK Gold repeats.

Wrapped within pristine sheets,
sunken eyes, drip fed, curtains pulled around him,
the colour gone from everything.

She used to talk about my school,
how my painting's going.
But now she asks why a small boy
is on her bed saying 'I love you Grandma'.

When all the little poems are finished, ask the children to practise reading their pieces. Then they should put them together and work out a way together to present a performance of their version of 'The Seven Ages of Man'. If another class is prepared to be an audience, or perhaps the whole school, you can provide a genuine theatrical few minutes. You might write an introduction yourself on the lines of the first four and a half lines. It might begin, for example, 'The world's a television serial/soap opera . . .'

Lesson Eighty-One: Petruchio is coming

The second passage could not be more different: prose not poetry, comic not serious, a buffoon described rather than a melancholic speaking. It's from 3.2.41–60 of *The Taming of the Shrew* . A character called Biondello is describing a man, Petruchio – the central character if not exactly a hero – turning up for his wedding. Petruchio is bizarrely dressed and riding an old sick horse:

BIONDELLO Why, Petruchio is coming in a new hat and an old jerkin, a pair of old breeches thrice turned, a pair of boots that have been candle cases, one buckled, another laced; an old rusty sword ta'en out of the town armoury, with a broken hilt and chapeless; with two broken points; his horse hipped, with an old mothy saddle and stirrups of no kindred, besides possessed with the glanders and like to mose in the chine, troubled with the lampass, infected with the fashions, full of windgalls, sped with spavins, rayed with yellows, past cure of the fives, stark spoiled with the staggers, begnawn with the bots, swayed in the back and shoulder-shotten, near-legged before and with a half-checked bit and a headstall of sheep's leather, which, being restrained to keep him from stumbling, hath been often burst, and now repaired with knots, one girth six times pieced, and a woman's crupper of velour, which hath two letters for her name fairly set down in studs, and here and there pieced with packthread.

 Read the lines to the children. Remember that you are aghast at the appearance of the groom. Try to make the speech funny. Nothing that Petruchio wears matches anything else ('a new hat and an old jerkin'). His boots are fastened in different ways. And his poor old horse: why bother about the obscure words? All of them, 'glanders', 'lampass', 'windgalls' and the rest are equine diseases.

Ask the children to write an imitation of this speech, bringing it up to date in clothing, and with a modern vehicle rather than a horse. They should do this all in one sentence – not only will this be close to the original, it will test their skill with commas, semi-colons and colons.

These pieces are by the apprentices:

Petruchio is coming, and a drunkard at that; his shirt ripped open with too-tight three-quarter length sleeves, the top pocket hanging ajar; his trousers ricked up to show fluorescent multicoloured mis-matched socks and worn-out too large sandals; he arrives on an ancient Vespa with only the letters E PA left and tyres that are flat on the floor, with an engine that is long gone, the handlebar a plastic plate, knee guard non-existent, the seat a pile of foam and the only reason it's moving is because he is using his feet.

Ellie

Petruchio is coming, in old jeans with ripped knees; old ciga-rettes falling out of the pocket of his stained tatty jacket; he has a shirt with no buttons and it's been sewn together with dirty green string; he's got his oldest wellington boots with holes in, big enough for mice to fit through; and . . . and his car . . . one front wheel's bigger than the other and the back wheels are as big as tractor wheels, and it grunts, and it roars, it bangs, it smokes, and it . . . oh, the smell, the smell! the smell seems to fill the world . . .

Xavier

Figure 14.1 Petruchio, by Xavier

Lesson Eighty-Two: The inmost part of you

Third, some lines from Hamlet. In the closet scene, the prince confronts his mother with the facts (as the ghost of his father has presented them): Claudius has murdered his brother, old Hamlet, and is living a sinful life with his brother's widow, Gertrude, to whom Hamlet is now speaking. At 3.4.19–20 he says:

You shall not go till I set you up a glass
Where you may see the inmost part of you.

A teacher once sent me some writing done by ten-year-olds that had been inspired by these lines. 'What', she had asked them, 'would a glass show that let you see the inmost part of you?' That is the activity here. Ask the children, what would be visible of you – your thoughts, emotions, visions, beliefs, enthusiasm, ambitions – if we could 'hold a mirror' up to you?

One child wrote:

The glass would reveal
a girl sitting at a computer
transfixed by the worldwide web,
a sea with bright blues and yellows in it.
The glass would reveal
the darkest storm cloud
but then it is washed away by the brightest biggest sun.
The glass would reveal
a crowd of people talking
about the lonely girl,

lonely because she is different.
The glass would reveal
a horse running around a tiny paddock
and then the gate being opened and the horse is free.

The glass would reveal
a giraffe, tall and solitary.
There is in me
a worn-out girl running in a race
at the front, with an aggressive look on her face . . .
a prison of words
full to the brim with things to say
never knowing where to start.
There is in me
a mainsail being hauled up the mast
powering the tiny dot . . .
a snowflake being ski-ed on
by a thousand on the biggest mountain you've ever seen.
There's a spelling book
with nothing written down . . .
a candle shrinking.

Anon.

Lesson Eighty-Three:
Poor naked wretches

This is the eighty-year-old King Lear caught in the centre of a 'pitiless storm'. He confesses that, during his reign, he has thought little of, and done nothing for, the 'houseless'. Two of his daughters have barred their gates against him and, as the rain pours down on him and the thunder roars, he begins to see what he had been blind to. Children see homeless people in their cities and towns almost every day, and this passage from *King Lear* (3.4.28–33) offers a chance for children to reflect on poverty by writing about it:

> Poor naked wretches, wheresoe'er you are
> That bide the pelting of this pitiless storm,
> How shall your houseless heads and unfed sides,
> Your looped and windowed raggedness defend you
> From seasons such as these? O I have ta'en
> Too little care of this . . .

Read these lines as well as you can, and ask the children to bring them up to date. Images of homelessness from the media, not hard to find, would help here. Like many of the lessons in this book, it provides opportunities for reflection on, and thinking about topics from Personal and Social Education. These are by ten-year-olds:

> Poor naked wretches around the world,
> those with no food or the wrong clothes,
> I shall give you warm blankets.
> I shall give you hot food and drink.

I will give you friendship, which is the most important of them all.
Poor naked wretches around the world
I will read you a bedtime story.
I will be there for you, just ask me for help
because I will not leave you there the rain
pouring on the top of your head.
I would rather this happened to me.

Gabi

The poor naked wretches, wherever you are in the world,
From the north to the south to the east to the west,
If you need sunshine may it come,
If there be drought may it be rain.
Oh the heartless storms wild hurricanes fly,
The poor figures under the trees,
Thou art trembling in the cold winds of winter
Where the only sound is the beating heart.
Oh all alone in the wild west wilderness
From the past to the present
Things haven't changed . . .

Abigail

Poor naked wretches wherever you are in a most unkind and
unhelpful world without any essential things, your lives hanging by
the thread, your poor bodies exposed to the elements, in a most
desperate situation, a race against time.

Elliott

Lesson Eighty-Four: The rose of youth

This is so simple. This line is from *Antony and Cleopatra* 3.13.20–21:

He wears the rose of youth upon him.

> Write the line up. Point out that it is built like this:
> Pronoun/verb/article (it could've been 'a' of course)/concrete noun/the word 'of'/abstract noun/preposition/another pronoun. A word or two about the distinction between concrete and proper nouns will probably be necessary: bring your hand down hard on a book and say, 'book', 'table' – two concrete nouns. Go to the window and call out what you see: 'roofs', 'bricks', 'wall', 'flower', 'cloud' – five concrete nouns. Then offer some abstract nouns – 'hope', 'love', 'hate', 'peace'. Ask the children to write lines on the same model. At first they shouldn't worry about 'making sense' – they should just obey the rule of the Shakespeare line. And they shouldn't use any of the words you've cited.

These children were nine and ten years old:

- *She wears the bud of babyhood about her.*
- *He flies the flag of fame in his hand.*
- *He wipes the dust of innocence off his shirt.*
- *He carries the tattered robe of earth with him.*

Lesson Eighty-Five: Shall I compare thee to a summer's day?

This lesson is here for teachers and children who want to push things further. Who want, in Phoebe's words (see below) to 'dig deep'.

Here is the octet, the first eight lines, of Shakespeare's Sonnet 18:

Shall I compare thee to a summer's day?
Thou art more lovely and more temperate:
Rough winds do shake the darling buds of May,
And summer's lease hath all too short a date;
Sometime too hot the eye of heaven shines,
And often is his gold complexion dimmed;
And every fair from fair sometime declines,
By chance, or nature's changing course untrimmed . . .

If you have a group of children who have felt the fire of language, whom you might label 'gifted' or 'able', and whom you know well, write a paraphrase of these lines, shamelessly muddying their precision with verbose phrases. What you come up with will be something like this:

Is it a good idea ['Shall I'] if I have thoughts of you as a period of twelve hours in the sunniest season? ['day' and 'summer']

You are more beautiful and comfortable to be with ['temperate']

Air moving harshly ['Rough winds'] makes those sweet growing parts, that will soon be petals, ['buds'] shiver

And the length of the warmest season is not so long as we would like.

Occasionally the sky's seeing organ ['the eye of heaven'] is excessively high-temperatured ['too hot']

And many times is his shiny yellow face ['gold complexion'] made less bright

And every lovely thing at some stage falls away from its loveliness

By good or bad luck [chance] or creation's altering progress uncropped . . .

This is pretty absurd, even ugly, of course: cumbersome in places – 'air moving harshly', indeed! And 'high-temperatured' is barely forgivable. But this travesty serves its purpose, and when the children edge closer to the Shakespeare by writing their versions of this version, it is a potent educational experience.

> Don't write it out on the whiteboard: give each child a copy, so that everyone is in a little world of his or her own for a while. Or, of course, you might use my example. Go through it with them. Avoid discussion for once – you want each child to come up with phrases uninfluenced by the others: that little world again. Ask them to write their own version, but with exact words, if possible, where your, or my, version is vague and wordy.

Although the extracts I give here were made by a group of 'able writers', they were not uniformly privileged in their backgrounds; but I knew them well, so with all of them there was a kind of friendship and a mutual respect. The first writer, though, was an exception: he had only been in the group for three afternoons over three weeks:

Can I think of you as half a day in summer?
You are more lovely and reassuring to be with.
                                        Kai

Shall I think of you as daylight in summer?
You are the best and safe, trusted to be with.
                                        Lottie

You are most wonderful and comfy to be around . . .
                                        Kimberley

Shakespeare's 'more temperate' became, through the veil of my 'more comfortable', variously these: 'more reassuring', 'trusted to be with' and (twice) 'more comfy'. I walked round the room as the children were working, and I could sense the intellectual and emotional energy in the first five minutes as they worked on this line.

> Shall I think for a moment of the days in summer
> When you are at your best?
>
> > Ellie

> My mind thinks only of you as the clock ticks away in summer.
> You will be clever and comfortable for an eternity...
> Time locked away for summer should be let out for an eternity of sunshine . . .
>
> > Lee

This last line has two amazingly felicitous phrases, the first fortuitously reminiscent of one of Philip Larkin's, his 'time laid up in store' in 'Love Songs in Age' (*Collected Poems*).

> . . . air moves harshly making sweet growing parts that'll soon be petals in a mid-Spring shake . . .
>
> > Mia

'A mid-Spring shake' – a spring-clean, what Mole is up to in the opening pages of *The Wind in the Willows*? No, just a happy version of l.3 ('Rough winds do shake the darling buds of May'). And I had written 'shiver' – Lauryn had discovered Shakespeare's word despite my distortion.

> . . . The time that we get in summer is not long enough,
> Sometimes the sky's beautiful sun is too hot . . .
> Every amazing piece at some time turns ugly . . .
>
> > Lauryn

. . . and many times his fiery face is silenced of its light . . .
Phoebe

Phoebe has coined a troubling and beautiful image with 'silenced of its light', with its synaesthesia – mixing of the senses, here hearing and sight.

. . . occasionally the sun burns down on us with a ferocious heat,
and many times its swirling, golden face is shrouded
And every beautiful thing at some time withers . . .
Katie

As every beautiful day drifts away to the sunset, a phrase I'm
going to say will be remembered for generations to come, even the
vibrant, glimmering sun will know . . .
Diana

This writer drifted further away from my paraphrase, and from the Shakespeare, and produced a long sentimental love poem. It ends 'I don't know if it was fate or destiny, but I'm glad I'm friends with you, and long live our friendship'. At the end of the session, when all the others had gone, and I was packing my bags, Diana was finishing copying this out. 'I'm going to give this to my mum' she said. Not my objective when I started the lesson. But once you set children free with something powerful, it is churlish to question how they use it. And of course Shakespeare's sonnet is a love poem to his friend.

It feels like an eternity of holding the gem-like colour . . .
Lee

Every beautiful thing at last turns bitter . . .
Ruby

. . . and withers, by fortune creation's altering course uncontrolled.
Katie

I asked the group how they had felt during the writing. There were murmurs of approval, and then Phoebe said 'I've been digging deep'. One of the best references I've ever had . . .

I then read the whole sonnet. The sextet reads:

But thy eternal summer shall not fade,
Nor lose possession of that fair thou ow'st,
Nor shall Death brag thou wand'rest in his shade,
When in eternal lines to time thou grow'st.
    So long as men can breathe or eyes can see,
    So long lives this, and this gives life to thee.

I said that it was a 'big-headed poem'. I ask them why I would say that: how is it arrogant? Ellie said, unhesitatingly, 'because he says the person won't die because of his poem'.

Notes

These paragraphs couldn't elbow their way into the main text.

Introduction

Note A: Teaching Shakespeare–an international context

It is possibly in non-civilized societies, as Soviet Russia was, that Shakespeare is most valued and most needed. It takes only a moment's thought to feel the power of Hamlet's line 'Something is rotten in the state of Denmark' when it is spoken on a stage or on a screen in a theatre that lives a precarious life under Stalin, or Brezhnev, or Vorster or Amin or Saddam; in a place where there are secret jails crammed with untried prisoners, or where there is a system in place for the removal of suspects to other countries for torture, a system so evil it can only be named with an obscure euphemism: rendition. One can readily imagine the effect a Zimbabwean production of *Richard III* might have on a people's thinking about tyranny; or how *Romeo and Juliet* might look to a society accustomed to seeing women as chattels. That society will be challenged to see that view enacted by Juliet's father as he threatens to drag his daughter to church on a sled in 3:5.

In an article in *the Guardian* (21.06.12) Gregory Doran and Rupert Goold recall producing *Titus Andronicus*, that bloodiest of the plays, in a South Africa that had just seen the end of apartheid. The hero's brother Marcus says at the end, 'O, let me teach you how to knit again / This scattered scorn into one knitted sheaf': 'truth and reconciliation' defined by Shakespeare in two iambic pentameters, four hundred years before the end of apartheid in South Africa. Then Doran relates a story from the apartheid years told by Anthony Sampson. A collected *Shakespeare* had been smuggled into the prison where Nelson Mandela was held, and some of the prisoners had underlined and signed their favourite passages. Mandela chose these lines from *Julius Caesar*: 'Cowards die many times before their deaths; / The valiant never taste of death but once . . .' Doran comments how that play 'gave the prisoners a deeper understanding of human courage and sacrifice . . . As Sampson wrote, "it reassured [them] that they were part of a universal drama"'.

As I write, a report appears in *the Guardian* for 16 July 2013:

Starting on 23 April 2014, the 450th anniversary of Shakespeare's birth, the [Globe theatre] will spend two years travelling . . . to visit every country on Earth – 205 in all.

The play they will take is *Hamlet*. The paper quotes the director Peter Brooke:

The six simplest words in the English language are 'to be or not to be' . . . There is hardly a corner of the planet where these words have not been translated. Even in English, those who can't speak the language will at once recognise the sound and exclaim: 'Shakespeare!'

So Shakespeare's words have the potential to speak to the whole world, and at all times. They are part of a project that all true educators are involved in, whether they know it or not: to keep the world civilised where it is, and to civilised it where it isn't. Deborah Warner put it like this: 'He's universal. His plays flow through the world's imagination on a daily basis . . . what Shakespeare does . . . is make you proud to be human (quoted in McCrum 'Who wrote Shakespeare . . .' *The Observer* 14 March 2010).

A Midsummer Night's Dream

Note B: Puck and Bottom

Each has an impact on his first appearance. Bottom is a prose-man, until he gets carried away with terrible stuff written for him, presumably, by Peter Quince. But Puck at his entry (2.1) speaks in verse, in flying rhyming couplets. He is that part of all of us that knows the air, as we do in pretence in childhood, and later in dreams, sometimes alarmingly; he is also a part of that element of human nature that we see in mischief-makers in folklore and literature almost everywhere: he is Anansi the Spider from the Caribbean, Brer Rabbit from the deep south of the United States, Finn McCool from Ireland; parts of him are William Brown and Dennis the Menace. The word 'mischief' could have been invented for him.

Where Puck soars, Bottom is grounded. Puck is air with touches of fire. As he famously says, 'I'll put a girdle round about the earth / In forty minutes!' Bottom is the element earth – though there is a touch of fire when he acts in his ebullient fantasising way.

Children in certain moods and at certain times see, consciously or subconsciously, something of themselves in both characters. Puck has their leaning towards mischief: there's often an air of 'What'll happen if I do this?' ('I'll be an auditor, / An actor too perhaps, if I see cause' he says to himself as he watches Peter Quince and his 'hempen homespuns' rehearse at 3.1.64). And Bottom can adopt a sulky tone that many of us probably remember from the playground. Just before 1.2.71, when he agrees to play Pyramus – and just Pyramus rather than Pyramus and Thisbe and the Lion as well ('Well, I will undertake it') he seems on the point of shouting 'It's not fair, I'm going home!'

These childlike qualities in Puck and Bottom don't only appeal to the children we teach. These characters will appeal to all of us who work with children, and who occasionally see our young selves mirrored in Shakespeare's characters' words – and the behaviour those words imply.

Note C: An eight-year-old boy writes under the influence of Puck—a brief case study on responding to children's writing

Floyd, to judge from how he started – the mixed big upper and lower case in his spelling of his name, the halting flow of his handwriting, the erratic slant of his lines – was the least fluent writer in his group. But he kept appearing at my side with a smile, a piece of paper, and a few written words.

I've brought home a smudgy photocopy, and it's next to my keyboard as I type. He has covered his sheet with tall letters, each one of which he seems to have laboured over. No letter is joined to the next, and each 'k' is written in three distinct strokes. Surprisingly, perhaps, for a struggling writer, most of the letters are formed in the conventional way – the *a*s loop anti-clockwise, for example, as handwriting experts say they should. All the *d*s and *p*s are written conventionally, too, but the *d*s with an oddly tall perpendicular stroke. Along the bottom are drawings of a house with the staircase visible, as in a cutaway model. There's also a little drawing of a sad human face behind bricks, rather like Malvolio after his imprisonment by Sir Toby and his friends in *Twelfth Night*.

The sheet is peppered with adult writing – the teacher's and mine – just to make it clear to any other possible readers, that 'pranck' really was 'prank' and 'sneck eff' was 'sneaky as'. Some of Floyd's other unconventional spellings are 'mistchiv', 'explod', 'drincks', 'resen', 'pepol', 'hoses,' (houses). The teacher has scribed 'banned from the spirit world'. Although I have been unable to transcribe some of the words, I have got it mostly right:

> *I am the God of mischief.*
> *I explode drinks*
> *in children's faces*
> *I prank babys I hide their things*
> *That's the reason I'm banned from the spirit world.*
> *I am as sneaky as God.*
> *I flood people's houses*
> *I blow up people's houses*
> *when they're away*
> *That's why I am banned from the spirit world*
> *To Be continued*
> *??????????*

What an interesting document this is. As well as the points I have made above, Floyd uses other means to communicate with his readers (that is, as far as he knows, his teacher and me). The note 'To Be continued' and the little flurry of question marks under it tell us, I suppose, that he has had enough of this experience for now, but that there may be at least a possibility of adding something another time. It also tells us that Floyd has had some experience of literature. I remember this phrase at the end of the episodes in the comics of my youth: he has presumably noted the phrase in his comics. Floyd has used vocabulary that is far from limited in range: 'banned from the spirit world' and 'sneaky as God' are positively daring.

It is obviously impossible to give this kind of attention to every piece of children's writing. But it would be a precious thing for each child-writer if it could happen, say, twice a term, and if it were followed by a serious one-to-one conversation that covered the content of the writing and, even more, the meaning of it, or the writer's intentions, before addressing clerical failures in punctuation and spelling.

Note D: More on teaching 'I'll follow you'

I often tell the children that I am going to say the lines again but, in an old-fashioned way. I am going to stop at the end of every phrase, and they are going to repeat that phrase exactly as I do. I often do this in a crescendo followed by a diminuendo: whispering the first phrases, rising to a low voice in the second line; getting louder in the third, arriving at a kind of controlled shout on 'A hog' . . . and then reducing the volume slowly to a whisper again on 'fire at every turn'.

There are other ways of playing with this speech which I also use: saying it in a different accent (my own childhood South London is, unsurprisingly, my first choice) and asking them to mimic me. This is all play, of course, but after about ten minutes many of the children have got the passage off by heart. Not by rote: that is a different and drearier matter.

I wrote above that the lines are playful. But they are also the words of a stalker: Puck's lines remind me of the Sting hit song of the early 1980s, a standard today to judge from the way teachers born in that decade and even after recognise it. In 'Every breath you take', a man is obsessively following someone, every move she makes. I have sometimes played this song to children before (never while) they write.

Note E: A note on doting in *A Midsummer Night's Dream*

What is called 'romantic love' – what a cynic might call sexual love with hearts and flowers grafted on – is out of the immediate experience of primary school children. That is why the sometimes childlike qualities of Puck and Bottom are much more important to them than the adolescent qualities of the four lovers. Neither Puck nor Bottom, as far as we know, has been 'in love', and Bottom is healthily sceptical about the whole business, as his dry comment to the besotted Titania shows. 'I love thee' she declares within a minute's acquaintance, and he replies with humdrum logic, or humdrum wisdom: 'Methinks, mistress, you should have little reason for that. And yet, to say the truth, reason and love keep little company together nowadays' (3.1.119). I think this line is the moral centre of the play.

But love, call it what you will – romance, sex, infatuation, obsession (the twentieth century word 'crush' comes to mind, especially when I think of how Demetrius and Lysander change so easily) – is, of course, the central theme of The *Dream*, and it would be foolish and dishonest to teach the play without acknowledging the fact. Famously, the course of it does not run smooth – as Lysander tells Hermia in 1.1 in one of the hundreds of Shakespeare's lines that have become idiomatic.

But is the play really about love? When I look through now at each of the relationships between, first, the betrothed (Theseus and Hippolyta), second, the married (Oberon and Titania) and finally the courting couples, one does not hold up much hope for any of these relationships. Theseus, as he blandly says on the first page of the script, has 'wooed' Hyppolita with his 'sword' and 'won her love doing [her] injuries'; and when he talks of wedding her 'in another key', that key is – 'pomp . . . triumph . . . revelling', Romeo he is not. I have seen him played to comic effect as an ex-military man nervously facing the demands of a political marriage. Hippolyta hardly opens her mouth throughout the play, and when she does in 1.1, her tone is formal, too.

Oberon and Titania spend most of the play at such loggerheads that Oberon allows his queen to become dangerously infatuated with an ass; and the lovers – the boys anyway – are at the whim of a dubious potion: what they experience under the influence of the potion it isn't so much love as doting. Crushes.

Frank Kermode points out in *Shakespeare's Language* that, while the word 'dote' appears eight times in the *Dream*, it is extremely rare elsewhere in Shakespeare. It is not an attractive word: derived from the Middle Dutch *doten*, it is most prominent in English in 'dotage', the foolish dithering of the senile, and in this play doting is not loving, even if it feels like it to the doter. It is the work merely of the eye rather than the mind, of the potion rather than the heart. It is, to say the least, foolish.

The Tempest

Note F: Shipwreck–some radio drama

For this lesson, reprise your performance of 1.1, and then hand out copies, preferably from a complete edition of the play. Arrange the children in groups of six of roughly mixed ability.

Each group should appoint a director who will also be an actor. That person then should hand out the parts of the Master, the Boatswain, King Alonso and the three courtiers, Antonio, Gonzalo and Sebastian. Each member of the group should read the script, and then the group should read it through together, talking about how each part should be done. Everyone should say the Mariners' line at 46 ('All lost! To prayers, to prayers, all lost') in a way that makes the panic of the characters clear, and everyone should contribute to (and improvise) the 'confused noise' a few lines later.

They should discuss the characters of each of the men: you might suggest that Gonzalo is gentle and optimistic – but what other adjectives can they think of to describe him? The Master and the Boatswain are (understandably) impatient – again, what other adjectives describe them? The very first words spoken by Sebastian, and Antonio's second speech, both composed of violent curses, give away the nature of these two characters.

The director should make notes of their findings, and each group should prepare a production of the scene for voices only – a radio play. The way they speak the lines should express what they have discovered about the characters.

The children should try to get the sounds of the storm in their pronunciation of words like 'roarers', 'howling', 'louder', 'bawling', etc. How can they convey a sense of confusion and noise without shouting all the way through? Some speeches might be spoken reflectively (Gonzalo's last two, for example) to provide contrast. Sometimes, to add to the sense of confusion, a speech should begin just before the previous one ends: but both speeches should be just about audible. The lines Sebastian and Antonio speak that I've mentioned above, for example, might be spoken with a venomous clarity, with the Boatswain's speech a contrasting roar ('Work you then') over the end of Sebastian's lines and the beginning of Antonio's.

Each group should have an opportunity to present their reading of the lines to the rest of the class and, if possible, to a bigger audience: another class, the school at assembly, parents, governors.

Later, the groups might prepare the scene again, with each child playing a different part.

Romeo and Juliet

Note G: The bawdry in *Romeo and Juliet*

Eric Partridge, in his admirable book (1947), says that 'Mercutio and the Nurse sex-spatter the most lyrically tragic of the plays'. Indeed, the first page of the

Cambridge School Shakespeare edition has eight obscene references. When a colleague taught this scene in a secondary school to what she described to me as a 'less able' set, one boy sniggered when she read Gregory's line 'Draw thy tool' – as boys – and girls – will. My colleague turned on him. What was she going to say? Would he grow up? How would she humiliate him in front of the class?

And she took all the wind wonderfully out of his sails: 'That's right! If you hear the word "tool" in this play, it almost certainly . . .' I imagined she faltered here, as I would have done . . . 'it almost certainly has a double meaning'. Well it does, and here it means 'penis'; or, more authentically, given the nature of the brawlers on stage at this point, it means 'prick'.

An option not open to primary school teachers, I suppose. But though the line between primary and secondary is clear if largely administrative, where the line is between child and adolescent, I don't know, and I would be hard put to speculate on it. The problem, for us with eight- to eleven-year-olds is that the play is funny – but that its humour is unrelentingly sexual.

Note H: Puns

There are plentiful puns in Romeo and Juliet, many of them – especially those spoken by the lowly characters in the first scene, or by Mercutio – obscene. But there are others. The first line puns on 'colliers' ('miners') and 'choler' ('anger'); Tybalt puns in l.57, 'What, art though drawn among these heartless hinds?', with 'heart' (a hart being a male deer, to be contrasted with 'hinds', female deer); Romeo puns ('sole/soul') in his third speech in 1.4. He doesn't want to dance, so he tells Mercutio and Benvolio:

> You have dancing shoes
> With nimble soles, I have a soul of lead . . .

and he puns again in his fourth speech in the same scene:

> I am too sore empierced with [Cupid's] shaft
> To soar with his light feathers, and so bound
> I cannot bound . . .

Mercutio and Romeo swap puns later (1.4.52–53):

> MERCUTIO . . . dreamers often lie.
> ROMEO In bed asleep.

Mercutio's grim pun 'a grave man' comes later (Chapter 12). Indeed, it is important to understand that, although today puns are mostly jokes, and weak ones at that, for Shakespeare they could be as serious as the murder of a king. Here are the Macbeths before and after the murder of Duncan:

> MACBETH . . . If the assassination . . . could catch
> With his surcease success.

> . . . LADY MACBETH If he do bleed,
> I'll gild the faces of the grooms withal,
> For it must seems their guilt.

Some children 'get' puns, many do not. Here a suggestion for those who do.

Point out these examples, and ask them to be keep their eyes open for more. Explain Lady Macbeth's pun: 'gild' (to paint) with 'guilt'. Suggest a pun of your own, and ask them if they can think of one. A teacher, quite shamelessly, offered a class: 'I was once very fond of a pencil, but it never led anywhere'. A better example: a boy was writing a riddle about a lion, and began his little poem 'My head is mainly gold'.

Note I: What is a sonnet? And an iambic pentameter?

The word 'sonnet' comes from the Italian for 'little sound'. A Shakespearean sonnet (there are other kinds that need not trouble us here) is made up like this: fourteen iambic pentameters, each made up of five feet, each foot being two syllables broadly like this in metre: da-DUM. So each line goes da-DUM da-DUM da-DUM da-DUM da-DUM.

The first eight lines – the octet – rhyme abab cdcd. The final six lines – the sestet–rhyme efef gg.

A pentameter is named after the Greek for 'five'. The children will be familiar with 'pent' in 'pentagon'. There are five athletic events in a pentathlon. A pentagram is a five-pointed star. And there are five feet in each line of a pentameter.

'Iamb' is originally from the Greek. It's metrical foot that is made up of two syllables, the second of which is stressed, as in the word 'Macbeth', 'galumph', 'grotesque', 'delight', 'invite': da-DUM da-DUM da-DUM da-DUM da-DUM.

Note J: More on Mercutio

For me, Mercutio mesmerises on every appearance. He does this in four ways, and three of them have the potential to mesmerise children into writing.

First, his language has such vigour: 'A plague on both your houses' he yells unforgettably – one of the many phrases in this play that are still sometimes on our tongues – when he realises that between them the Montagues and the Capulets have killed him. His Queen Mab speech in 1.4 paints word pictures of such wild clarity that they can entrance many a ten-year-old. Indeed, whenever he appears, his wordplay lights up both the stage and the page.

The second reason for the power of Mercutio's spell is the way his language drives like a sword's point into the heart of much of the main subject of the play. And I don't mean love: Mercutio is unforgiving in his disrespect for any hearts and flowers stuff. Like that very different character, Bottom, he knows that 'reason and love keep little company together nowadays' (The *Dream* 3.1.120).

No, he is central in the development of a theme that is loud, if ragged, at the very beginning of the play when we are in the company of Capulet's servants, one that builds in a crescendo to Mercutio's and Tybalt's deaths, and then threatens to deafen us in Juliet's tomb in the final act. That theme is quarrelling. One line of Mercutio's, 'Poor Romeo, he is already dead, stabbed with a white wench's black eye' (2.4.13), packs references to three of the play's themes into one line: violence, death . . . and love. In that order.

The third reason for this spell-casting, for me anyway, is that he dies about halfway through the play: it's an absorbing puzzle. Why does this happen? It has been suggested that Shakespeare, still a young writer, has suddenly realised that this character, with his vigour and his poetry, is threatening Romeo's status as the main male focus of the play. The mature Shakespeare might have found a way to quieten Mercutio down without depriving him of his vigour; might even have found for him a role in the Friar part of the story. But he killed him. What might Mercutio have done had he survived? One can only imagine what his reaction would have been to the Friar's scheming, and to the lovers' deaths.

A further point may be unhelpful in practical terms for the book I am writing, but it would be irresponsible to not mention it because it might colour our teaching of his lines. It is there just behind the Queen Mab speech and in his teasing of Romeo: his florid obscenity. 'Peace, peace, Mercutio, peace!' Romeo pleads at 1.4.95–96, in an attempt to calm Mercutio while he is full flood about 'maids [lying] . . . on their backs'.

It is a loss to our teaching that this bawdry rules most of Mercutio's lines out of court in primary schools. Look at lines like those at 2.1.17–20 and 24–26, which would have been riotously and raucously received in the pit. They have such creativity in their filth; they give the lie so eloquently to the tiresome 'Wonderful-heritage-that-the-Bard-or-should-I-say-the Swan-of-Avon—bequeaths-us' school of thought. They have a vital (from the Latin *vita* 'life') function in the play: this story needs something to offset its purity, and to show us that there is filth and quarrelling in this world even where there is redeeming purity; or, to see it from the other end of the telescope, that there is redeeming purity in this world of filth and quarrelling. Mercutio performs this function with Romeo, as the Nurse does with Juliet (1.3).

And finally: is it possible that Mercutio is jealous of anyone, whether Rosaline or Juliet, who holds Romeo's attention? That he loves Romeo? Critics have suggested that there might be a gay subtext, and to my ear there is certainly a kind of camp vivacity in the Queen Mab speech. And this speech, over fifty lines long, which seems to ignore Benvolio and the other people on stage, is easily read as an attempt to hold Romeo, to keep him where he is.

References

Bate, J. (1997) *The Genius of Shakespeare.* London: Picador.

Bloom, H. (1999) *Shakespeare: The Invention of the Human.* London: Fourth Estate.

Brownjohn, S. (1982) *What Rhymes with Secret?* London: Hodder and Stoughton.

Doran, G. and Goold, R. (2012) Power and Glory, *the Guardian.* 20 June 2012. G2 section, p. 16.

Gray, M. (1984) *A Dictionary of Literary Terms.* Harlow: Longman

Heaney, S. (1966) *Death of a Naturalist.* London: Faber.

Kermode, F. (2000) *Shakespeare's Language.* London: Allen Lane/The Penguin Press.

Lamb, C. and Lamb, M. (1994 [1807]) Tales from *Shakespeare.* Ware: Wordsworth Editions Limited.

Larkin, P. (1988) *Collected Poems* ed. Anthony Thwaite. London: Faber and Marvell Press.

McCrum, R. (2010) 'Who wrote Shakespeare ...' *The Observer.* 14 March 2010. The New Review section, pp. 18–21.

Nabokov, V. (1980) *Lectures on Literature* ed. Fredson Bowers. London: Picador.

National Geographic (2004) *In Focus: National Geographic's Greatest Photographs.*

Onions, C. T. (1919) *A Shakespeare Glossary.* Oxford: Clarendon Press.

Partridge, E. (1947) *Shakespeare's Bawdy.* London: Routledge.

Sedgwick, F. (1999) *Shakespeare and the Young Writer.* London: Routledge.

Sedgwick, F. (2011) *Inspiring Children to Read and Write for Pleasure.* London: Routledge.

Sellers, S. (ed.) (1991) *Taking Reality by Surprise: Writing for Pleasure and Publication.* London: The Woman's Press.

Shorter Oxford English Dictionary (1973 third edition). Oxford: Oxford University Press.

Cambridge School Shakespeare:

A Midsummer Night's Dream (1992) eds. Linda Buckle and Paul Kelley
The Tempest (1995) ed. Rex Gibson
Romeo and Juliet (1992) ed. Rex Gibson

Macmillan Shakespeare

A Midsummer Night's Dream (2008) eds Jonathan Bate and Eric Rasmussen
Romeo and Juliet (2009) eds Jonathan Bate and Eric Rasmussen

Index

Note: entries here on the main three plays dealt with in this book – *A Midsummer Night's Dream, The Tempest* and *Romeo and Juliet* – do not include the main sections devoted to them.

TEACHING CREATIVE WRITING IN THE PRIMARY SCHOOL: DELIGHT, ENTICE, INSPIRE!

Julie MacLusky & Robyn Cox

978-0-335-24279-5 (Paperback)
September 2011

This book aims to support and develop creative writing activity in the primary curriculum, offering a balanced mix of both theoretical background and practical writing ideas. The book provides various exercises that will help develop creative writing skills, from creating an engaging character to delivering a satisfying ending. The structured and well-tested exercises will help to develop fundamental, transferable tools of story telling that will improve pupil's confidence in all areas of writing.

Key features:
- Providing detailed curriculum links to the National Strategy strands and outcomes
- 20 creative writing templates for activities that can be incorporated into many different areas of classroom teaching

www.openup.co.uk